SOME ASPECTS OF SIN

SOME ASPECTS OF SIN

THREE COURSES OF LENT SERMONS

PREACHED IN THE

CATHEDRALS OF ST. PAUL'S AND LINCOLN

AND IN THE

CHAPEL OF KEBLE COLLEGE, OXFORD

BY THE LATE

AUBREY L. MOORE, M.A.

HONORARY CANON OF CHRIST CHURCH
EXAMINING CHAPLAIN TO THE LATE AND PRESENT BISHOPS OF OXFORD
FELLOW TUTOR AND DEAN OF DIVINITY OF MAGDALENE COLLEGE
AND TUTOR OF KEBLE COLLEGE, OXFORD

THIRD EDITION

London
PERCIVAL & CO.
1893

NOTE

THE sermons, here offered to the public, were found among the deceased writer's papers, and they have been printed as they were found,—even with the expressions, obviously chosen for oral delivery. Regrets will naturally be felt that the book could not receive the revising touch of "the vanished hand;" but, to the hearers of the sermons, it is believed, it will be some compensation to have them reproduced in all their original force and freshness.

D. M.

CONTENTS

I. LENTEN LESSONS.

Addresses delivered in the Chapel of Keble College, in Lent, 1882

II. SOME ASPECTS OF SIN.

Addresses delivered in St. Paul's Cathedral, in Lent, 1886.

III. THE DISCIPLES AND THEIR LORD.

Sermons in Lincoln Cathedral, in Holy Week, 1889.

I.

COURSE OF FIVE SERMONS

Preached in the Chapel of Keble College, Oxford
in Lent, 1882

on

LENTEN LESSONS

I.

WATCHFULNESS.

"Watch ye, stand fast in the faith, quit you like men, be strong. Let all your things be done with charity."—1 COR. xvi. 13, 14.

THE object of these Lenten Addresses is not to lay before you any new views as to those great subjects which at such a time seem appropriate, nor even to attempt to defend and justify the teaching of Christ's Holy Church about them. I have set before myself a much simpler task, and yet one which, by God's grace, may be made far from useless even to those of us who have advanced furthest in the spiritual life, or are best able to grapple with the problems which are ever present in it. We who meet in this chapel day after day, to worship the One Lord, differ no doubt socially; and yet there are other differences which mark us off far more sharply from one another. Intellectual differences, in such a society as ours, are easily recognized, and as easily acquiesced in. Differences in spiritual matters must necessarily be a more secret thing known only to Him Who seeth not as man seeth, but seeth the hearts. God looks down upon us who worship here, and He sees—what? He sees these, fighting in a battle which their nearest friends know nothing of. He sees those, almost ready to give up the struggle in despair. Others, again—He sees, and knows who they are—perhaps, all unconsciously, are destroying their own powers of resistance, parleying treacherously with the foe instead of fighting, giving way step by step, often in the futile hope that the lost ground may be recovered by a sudden sally at some opportunity which never comes. Others, again, little known, perhaps little esteemed, holding no high place in the competition for intellectual distinction, God sees walking in the paths of holy obedience —I had almost said saintliness—in the world, not of the world, quite unfitted to meet or even understand the difficulties which sadden so many a life, and yet already seeing something of the vision of God which we would gladly see.

In the presence of these and innumerable other differences, is it possible to speak so as to help many? Only, I believe (and this is my apology for choosing the course I have chosen), only by going back to very simple truths, things that we all know so well that they have become almost meaningless, only by piercing through to that which is common to us as man, the fact of sinfulness. "All have sinned, and come short of the glory of God." "There is none righteous." In that sad truth, S. Paul found common ground for heathen and for Jew. In that truth, those differences I have spoken of shrink into littleness, and tend to disappear altogether.

"All have sinned." May I assume anything more? Yes. I must assume that while we all stand on that common ground as sinners before God, we also stand on common ground as professing Christians—men who at least have had the opportunity of knowing what God has done to bridge over the gulf between us and Him; who have at least had put before them the truth, that if we are but ordinary men, with ordinary temptations, and guilty only of ordinary sins, it is yet ours to use those means of reconciliation and recovery which we may dare to call ordinary too.

May I not go one step further, and assume that you are, every one of you, at least desirous of doing right? I will not believe that there is one among us, even amongst those who are furthest removed from the Christian faith and the Christian life, who is not conscious that there is within him and around him a body of death which he would fain overcome or be delivered from. I will not believe that there is one so intellectually shallow, or so morally inert, as to acquiesce in that superficial view that all the seething mass of moral corruption has no existence but in the fancy of those who wish to justify the existence of a priestly caste.

At the same time, speaking in this place, and to this audience, I must openly and plainly assume the attitude of a Christian priest. To build up from the beginning the Christian system would be as unnecessary and impossible for me, as it would be unnecessary for most of you. I am speaking on practical, not speculative, questions. I am assuming that you, no less than I myself, are anxious for any hints that may help us in the Christian warfare.

For the five addresses it has therefore been suggested to me that I should take those injunctions of S. Paul to the Corinthians, which seem to gather up at least the most important duties of the Christian warrior: "Watch ye. Stand fast in the faith. Quit you like men. Be strong. Let all your things be done with charity." I say the Christian "warrior," because the warnings seem, like so many of S. Paul's sayings, to have had a definite reference to a soldier's duties. Vigilance, steadfastness, manliness, strength, and that which is distinctive of the soldier of the Cross—*love*, or *charity*.

"Watch ye." That is the first charge to the Christian soldier; and it is a charge repeated by nearly every one of the New Testament writers. "Watch and pray." "What I say unto you, I say unto all, Watch." "Blessed is he whom the Lord, when He cometh, shall find watching." These words of the Master, recorded by the Evangelists, are repeated again and again by His other followers. "Be sober," says S. Peter, "be vigilant; because your adversary the devil, as a roaring lion, walketh about, seeking whom he may devour." S. John again, in the Revelation, repeats the blessing which his Lord had long before pronounced, "Blessed is he that watcheth." We need not multiply, as we easily might, the passages which charge us to be watchful.

But what does watchfulness mean? It certainly, I think, always implies an effort, and therefore something of self-denial, for a special purpose; and the form in which that self-denial shows itself is in *the being wakeful when we are inclined to sleep.* They who watch by the sick-bed, no less than the sentinel who watches at his post, deny themselves, do violence to natural inclinations, though love, or the imperious sense of duty, makes such self-denial almost unconscious.

Watchfulness, then, as the first of the Christian soldier's duties, will imply *self-denial, self-discipline effort.* This even the disciples, in spite of the Master's words, did not realize at once. As long as He was with them, danger seemed far removed; and even when the end was near, and the forces of the enemy were gathering round, and the traitor was close at hand, they were overcome with sleep, and only roused at that sad reproval, "What, could ye not watch with Me one hour?" Afterwards the infant Church, surrounded as it was by persecuting and malicious foes, learned at least to *watch.* Is the need less now? Are the forces of evil fewer or less bitter? Are we stronger to resist? Has the tempter forgotten his old tactics? Or have we such weapons of precision that we can afford to laugh at him? Men act as if it were so. They slip through life in a languid, flaccid, nerveless way. We see it again and again. It is not that they are bad or vicious. They would repudiate at once the wish to be evil; but there is a miserable *laisser-faire* in the ordering of life. They don't make terms with the enemy, but they leave the gates open, if at the moment they see no enemy near. And yet can we ever say the enemy of our soul's life is not near? See what a thoroughfare our heart is at every hour. At every instant there are fresh arrivals and departures by the five great gates, as Bunyan calls them—the five senses, by which strangers enter—and who will count the side gates? Take the trouble to review the rapid changes of thought and feeling which you have experienced in the course of a few minutes' conversation. A chance word is spoken, and self is up in arms; our pride is hurt, and we answer angrily, or we say something smart at a grievous loss of Christian charity, or something amusing at the price of truth, or something witty at the expense of sacred things, or something clever to the great harm of purity. And if we are alone, still there is the ceaseless coming and going of thoughts, some, no doubt, direct from the throne of God, as angels sent to purify and cleanse His dwelling; yet some great thoughts there are which come but to defile and pollute and stain. Or, think again of the daily and hourly danger to which we are exposed by the very atmosphere in which we live—the literature of the day, the companions we are brought into contact with, the general tone of society. I suppose no one is so optimistic as to think that these are permeated by the Christian spirit. And yet we move amongst them without watchfulness; and that when we know that in our own nature there is something which corresponds only too readily to the touch of outside evil. We find our worst self reflected in others, or in the novels which only picture others, and we forget that we have a higher and a better self that we must guard at every cost. We move freely amidst a general conflagration, while the very garment that we wear is steeped in that which is ready to take fire; or we live in air reeking with infection which our state is specially open to, and yet we do not watch, and yet we are light-hearted, and take things as they come, and then we wonder that we are the victims of our own folly. Unbelief, impurity, carelessness of truth, disregard of honesty, contempt for high ideals in life, evil in every form and every disguise, surround us constantly.

What precautions are we taking? We are reasonable men, foreseeing men. We can use the past to guide us in the future. What has our boasted experience taught us?

I. I think it is a fact of experience, if anything is, that while there are many temptations which beset us all, there is generally one which our own individual nature is specially inclined to; which, if we give way to it, seems, as it were, to swallow up all other temptations. At least, if we examine the other temptations, they seem all to converge on the one point; their distinctive character is lost in that of the "besetting sin," just as when the plague raged at Athens, all other diseases, we are told, seemed to lead up to and to end in it. What that besetting sin is, each must find out for himself, and having found it out, *watch.* Watch, not merely against that old besetting sin, but against everything which, in however indirect a way, is associated with it. It may be something quite innocent in itself, quite harmless to another, whose special temptation is of another kind.

For *you* it is fraught with deadly peril. *Watch*, then, as a soldier on duty, and sound the alarm at once It may be only as the light glancing on an enemy's gun; the enemy may flee directly he is observed; but don't wait to make sure till he gets near enough to master your weapon. If the enemy has once gained an entrance, he will loiter about the old breach, and wait his opportunity. He will not give us time to rebuild the walls—we can but patch them up; and there must always be a weakness there, and the enemy knows it. An attack which might be easily repelled elsewhere will be fatal here. You know what I mean; you know well if you have ever struggled against evil. The old indulged sin sends its fibres down deep into our very being, and it is long before we can be sure that, though torn up by the roots, it may not have left in the ground that which under favourable conditions will grow again. We may break the bad habit, but there is the old weakness, the old craving, the old desire for sin, whether sensual or refined, which for us means spiritual death. Never make another's temptations the measure of your own, or another's strength the gauge of yours; but *watch.*

II. Again, experience has taught us that in the spiritual combat *we cannot be too watchful against those sins which we think we have no temptation to commit.* It is by these that the penitent too often falls. S. Peter knew he was impetuous and impulsive and impatient; but unfaithful to his Lord he *could* not be. "Though I should die with Thee, yet will I not deny Thee." And e'er the cock crowed, he wept bitterly over a bitter fall. Satan may be a very wicked being, but he is a wonderfully good general. He is neither omnipotent nor omniscient, nor omnipresent, but he can use his opportunities. He will not long waste his power on the part which you know is weak, where all your sentries have been doubled, but he will turn to that where you think yourself secure, where you never have been attacked. So it was that the virgin fortress of Babylon fell before the conquering Cyrus. The walls were manned, the sentinels were at their posts, every attack failed; yet secretly—no watch was set where Euphrates and the brazen gates seemed to mock at danger—the enemy entered and surprised the citadel. Never say to yourselves, as we are so ready to say, Ah, I have my faults and my besetting sins, but at least, *this* will never be one. I feel no inclination to *that* sin. When such a thought suggests itself, then, if ever, watch against that very sin. It is there that the enemy is about to attack.

III. Again, experience has taught us to be especially watchful when any special effort has been made, or any victory won by the power of God in us, when we have felt God's nearness, and been for the moment lifted up above the ordinary life of conflict. At such a season as that on which we enter to-day,[1] when many new resolutions are being made, new efforts to struggle manfully against evil, there is special need of watchfulness. Our greatest sins often follow closely

[1] Ash Wednesday.

on our highest resolutions, simply because new efforts against the enemy always stir up the enemy to new efforts against us. The very making of a resolution, and offering it to God, is an appeal against the strong one to Him Who is "stronger than the strong." Even in our Blessed Lord's case, there seems to have been a mysterious connection between His fasting and His temptation. For fasting, self-restraint, self-discipline, is a preparing the soul for fight, a strengthening it against the moment of trial, and the devil fears it—feels that each act of self-restraint gives strength to what he would overcome, and his only hope is in immediate attack. The soul that fights may be overcome; the soul that prays, *never.* The sinner who loves his sin is safe in the bondage of evil,—the sinner who resolves in God's strength to fight, has already struck a blow for liberty.

And yet, for we are not ignorant of his devices, the evil one will sometimes follow a different plan. Instead of attacking your resolution, he will praise you for it, compliment you, as it were, on the strength you have shown, soothe you to sleep like Samson in Delilah's lap, and then rob you of that in which your strength lay, your trust in God. He will make a feigned retreat, as if we had vanquished him. We are left for a moment in all the bliss of restored union with God, and peace from external assaults. *Watch* then. Be doubly watchful then. We are never in such danger as when all things say "peace;" never safe except while we are conscious of present danger. The enemy never does in this life give up his attempts, except for a time, to get us into a state of false security. Again and again the old story, legend if you will, of the Wooden Horse is repeated in our lives. The enemy that has besieged us so long seems to depart. We are proud of our victory; we think to spoil the deserted camp. And the very spoil is tainted, carries within it hidden treachery, to take us unawares. The word, the thought, which we open the gate to admit, which we fancied was a proof of our victory, which, at least, now the enemy is gone, cannot be dangerous, is doomed to be the means of our fall. The seemingly harmless thought is received into the soul, and begets desire; and desire bears its fruit in sin; and sin, "when it is perfected, bringeth forth death." Under cover of the night, the enemy has returned, the traitor hand has opened the gates, and the city is lost.

So much I have said as to the duty of watching the enemy and his tactics. The other kind of watching I can but hint at. It is not enough to watch the enemy, we must watch ourselves. Mere opportunity does not make sin, if there is not consent of the will to evil. Therefore, watch yourselves—your conscience, that it be sensitive, ready to vibrate to the touch of God; your practice, that it be right, truly conformed to the law of God; your motives, that they are pure, seeking first and before all the will of God; your affections, that they stretch ever upwards and onwards till they rest in God.

"Keep thine heart," says the Wise Man, "above all keeping;"—the heart, not the head, for the heart, in Bible language, is the seat of the affections. Keep them, and you keep all. In worldly affairs, we know how all-important it is to keep cool and collected, to be, as we say, clear-headed, not to be misled by false arguments. In the spiritual life, the arguments of the great deceiver are addressed not to the head, but to the heart. Rarely, if ever, does Satan put intellectual difficulties in our way, unless he has prepared us for them by temptations addressed to the heart. At least, if he assails your reason, it is only that he may gain an entrance to, or establish himself more firmly in your heart. For your heart is God's. Christ died to win it back to God. "Give Me thine heart," He cries, and it is the heart which instinctively bids us answer—Lord, Thou hast made me for Thyself. My heart knoweth no rest till it attain to Thee.

II.

STEADFASTNESS IN FAITH.

"Watch ye, stand fast in the faith, quit you like men, be strong. Let all your things be done with charity."—I COR. xvi. 13, 14.

"STAND fast in the faith." What faith? The faith once delivered to the saints,[1] the faith from which in every age some have erred,[2] while some have held it fast;[3] the faith which some have fought for,[4] and some have betrayed;[5] the faith which in ancient days was gathered up in a form[6] or outline for the guidance of after ages, as the "profession"[7] of the Church's belief. That is the faith in which we are bidden to stand fast.

And we must notice at the outset that standing fast in the faith implies an exercise of the *will*, not of the *reason*. We are not bidden to seek something we have not, but to hold fast that which we have. It implies, like watchfulness, an effort, and a present power working against us. Here again, then, we see that it is a practical, not a speculative, question we have to deal with—not how is definiteness possible in such high, mysterious matters? how can human

[1] Jude 3. [2] I Tim. vi. 10, 21.
[3] Rev. ii. 13; Heb. x. 23. [4] I Tim. xi. 12.
[5] I Tim. i. 8. [6] 2 Tim. i. 13. [7] Heb. x. 23.

language express, or human thought realize, truths which touch the very nature of God, and His purposes in the Incarnation? but how can we hold fast against the enemy the heritage of truth which by God's grace is ours?

Again, we notice that standing fast in the faith implies, not keeping this and rejecting that, or retaining this and modifying or recasting that, but keeping in its definiteness and completeness the whole truth of God, as revealed to the Christian Church. Indeed, I may say, the whole matter circles round that one word "definiteness." Can we dare to stand fast in the definite faith which the Apostles held, and fearlessly to declare it to others? The two things must go together, though some try to separate them. We must *believe definitely* that we may run, not as uncertainly; we must *definitely declare our belief* for the sake of others, lest, if our trumpet give an uncertain sound, they know not how to prepare themselves for the battle. There are, I said, some who separate these two duties, who hold some doctrines of our faith to be "lawful, but not expedient," defensible, and even true, but better kept in the background,—either because people generally are not prepared to receive them, or because the truths themselves are out of harmony with the feelings of the age. Of these two reasons, sometimes alleged for keeping back any part of God's revelation, we can only say that the first is *dangerous*, and the second is too often *cowardly*. Who save God Himself can tell who is fit and who is not fit to receive the mysteries of the kingdom?

May not the truths which are least in harmony with the age in which we live, be just the truths which Christians are charged to hold forth before an unbelieving world? Such reasons are often advanced with reference to the solemn warnings of the Athanasian Creed, or the awful doctrine of eternal punishment. They are true, some will say, but had better not be given too prominent a place in the present state of religious feeling. Such a statement, if it does not conceal, as is too often the case, a half-belief which is no belief, in the truths themselves, is at least hard to reconcile with the duty of one who is charged on his allegiance to "stand fast in the faith."

I must assume, then, without further argument, that we are earnestly intending to teach definitely what we definitely believe; and, by this assumption, our subject becomes narrowed down to *definiteness of belief*.

Now, all real faith is definite faith. You can no more have faith in what is only a balance of probabilities than you can stand upon a rolling ball. But the word "faith," like most words which have taken their place in ordinary language, is in danger of losing its meaning. Faith, theologically, is the correlative of truth, truth absolute,[1] truth for all. Faith, popularly, often means little else than the more or less indefinite views which men hold on subjects beyond the range of knowledge. Now, this latter faith, if faith it can be called, has no enemies; for it is not worth fighting against. The most ardent

[1] Ὅπερ ἐστι ἓν καὶ ταὐτὸ πᾶσιν.

champion of scientific or philosophic truth can hardly refuse to allow a man to fill up with his private fancies, be they original or borrowed, the unclaimed territory of the scientifically unknown. But the moment Faith, the gift of God, comes before the world with a revelation of truth, truth definite and absolute, affecting those great realities—God, the soul, and immortality—then at once all the powers of the world are leagued against it. It is mere dogmatism, or the stolid and irrational clinging to old-world fancies, or it is an anachronism which brings the Schoolman's subtleties into the light of the nineteenth century. Or the objections will take a more specious form. Have your own definite beliefs, if you will, in these high and mysterious matters, but don't be so narrow-minded and intolerant as to wish others to believe them. Do allow men the right of private judgment—in other words, believe what you will, only do not tell us that what you believe is *true*.

It is here that Christian faith, clear and definite, because it is real, is brought into sharp antagonism with the tendencies of our age. Probably never had the opponents of definite faith a longer or more variously constituted army.

I. For, first, the tendency of the present century—the spirit of the age, as some would call it—is an insatiable craving for unity. The last century was a century of sharp divisions and distinctions; now we must have unity at any price. And all the old landmarks are being swept away. We cannot tolerate hard-and-fast lines. To our wisdom, they savour of ignorance or imperfect knowledge. Everything shades off into something else; everything higher is evolved, so the phrase goes, from something lower. There are no breaks, no old-fashioned distinctions between animal and vegetable, hardly between animate and inanimate;[1] certainly none between reason and instinct, man and brute; at least it is a difference in degree and not in kind. And we read history so wisely. The great events, revolutions, reformations, what not? which excited the wonder of our forefathers, we can trace them all "in the germ," and should have been very much surprised if they had not taken place. And when a great man appears upon the world's stage, we see in him, say he was, "the product of his times." In former days he was thought a miracle, we know that he is part of the reign of law. . . . And in direct antagonism to this easy-flowing and satisfactory philosophy, the truths of the Christian faith come out in sharp, clear, uncompromising definiteness. The sharp lines of separation are as sharp as ever, the separation eternal and unchanging between the Church and the world, the flesh and the Spirit, God and Mammon, those who hold, and those who reject the Catholic Faith. Sharp, clear, and uncompromising are the statements which the Church repeats as to the doctrine of the Holy Trinity, and the Incarnation of the Son of God, the greatest of mysteries, and the greatest of miracles, for which the philosophy of the day has no parallel and no place. Definite faith is something quite out of harmony with the advanced

[1] Cf. the Archebiosis controversy.

thought of the day, whether it follow the lines of materialism or pantheism.

II. Then, again, the widely diffused education of our day has incidentally, and not as a necessary consequence, contributed to the prevailing hatred of definiteness. For education shows us the many-sidedness of truth, shows us how rarely it can be comprehended in a formula. And we are prejudiced against all short and easy methods of proof or refutation, and we see that ignorance for the most part is content with one side of a question, and is intolerant of any view except its own. And we have caught from the critics a hatred of dogmatism, and if we are inclined to halt between two opinions, it is very comforting to know on good authority that there must be a great deal to be said on both sides. And gradually we come to think that it is almost a proof of higher culture not to be very certain about what we believe and speak, "with bated breath and whispering humbleness," of the creeds and dogmas which we are bound to hold fast.

III. I am afraid, too, that this dislike of clear and definite beliefs is unconsciously countenanced by many who in their hearts would be little inclined to favour it. There are many earnest-minded Christians who are so morbidly afraid of a mere barren belief that they sometimes allow themselves to talk as if to hold fast any form of sound words must be formalism, as if, in fact, the belief in a creed were rather dangerous than helpful. It is true, of course, as we all know well, that a right creed cannot save a man, and that when the bridegroom comes, many may be found with lamps that have no oil ; but surely, if we discard our lamp, much of the precious oil we have may be lost.

Now, in face of these, and many other opposing forces, what is our duty as Christian warriors ? Clearly it is to stand fast in the faith. Compromise has no place in the Christian view of truth. "Let God be true, and every man a liar," rather than that one jot or tittle of revealed truth should be explained away, or kept in abeyance, in deference to the changing opinions of men.

The Church, the one body in which the one Spirit dwells, the Church which S. Paul scruples not to call "the pillar and ground of the truth," has committed to us a sacred deposit: the three Creeds to be our Rule of Faith, the Holy Scriptures to be our Rule of Life ; and this sacred deposit we must keep. We reject, as Christians, the assumptions of a higher criticism which would correct and emend the Inspired Word of God ; we reject as Christians that empirical theology which would recast, as some would say, "rehabilitate," the belief of the undivided Church. The Creeds, remember, are our "scientific frontier," which the soldiers in Christ's army must die to defend. To most of us, those definitions of faith must remain as ultimate facts. "This is the Catholic Faith." The soldier's duty is to defend his country, not coolly to discuss with the enemy the right of original possession. It is a grievous mistake to suppose that every tyro, with his Bible in his hand, may attempt to recast, or even to eradicate, those deep and mysterious truths which holy men of old, led by the Spirit of God, wrought out by prayer and fasting. The definiteness and precision of these scientific formularies has been the rock against which antichristian thought has broken. In vain has it disguised its disappointment under the cloke of anxiety for spiritual religion, and the fear lest, as a writer in "Essays and Reviews" words it, "a godless orthodoxy should extinguish religious thought," and nothing should be left in the Church of England but "the formulæ of past thinkings which have lost all sense of any kind." In vain does it set its hope for the future in the fact that these distinctions of theology are beginning to fade away.[1] Never, while faith lives in the Church of England, can theology become what the rationalist would have it be, "a nimbus of golden mist." Never can the sharp, definite outlines of Catholic Truth disappear in a beautiful indefiniteness, in which, as in one of Turner's pictures, heaven and earth are blended, and the horizon lost in a strange mysterious haze. Never till faith is dead, and then, if that day ever comes, for a little while will mistiness be deemed the mother of wisdom, and men will seek to guide us (I use the words of the "Apologia") "through the channel of no-meaning, between the Scylla and Charybdis of Aye and No," till, sharp and clear, new lines are seen appearing through the mist, the definite outlines of a godless, Christless creed.

The indefinite faith is a transitional phase. You

[1] From "The Age and the Gospel," Hulsean Lectures, 1865, by Rev. D. Moore.

cannot rest in it. But once allow yourselves to be seduced so far, and the ordinary temptations of manhood will do the rest. You will have a definite creed again—the creed of selfishness and sin. *God* or *self*. It must be one or the other towards which you gravitate, though for a time you are attracted by both. Don't think that you can live the Christian life without the Christian motive, or show forth the Christian virtues while you discard the Christian verities. It is one of the commonest baits by which men are drawn from their steadfastness. "Take the morality and leave the doctrines," it is said. We are all agreed that the moral ideal of the Christian is a good one. Why hamper it by metaphysical and theological teaching which is a survival of an age that is gone? Because a supernatural life must be the result of a supernatural force, at least so far as we have got hitherto, the much-desired natural force which is to do the work is still to be discovered. We are told that now we are outgrowing religion, the secularization of morals necessarily follows.[1] Till that new and scientific, *i.e.* naturalistic, basis be found, we must expect "a moral interregnum,"[2] because morality cannot stand alone. How far a people that has passed through a moral interregnum will be capable, even with a basis yet to be discovered, of rebuilding the fabric of morals, I must leave you to imagine. The interest of the question for our present purpose

[1] See Goldwin Smith's "Review of 'Data of Ethics'' (*Contemporary Review*).

[2] Spencer's "Data of Ethics," pref.

is this, that on mere prudential grounds, and apart from the higher questions involved, we have strong motives for standing fast in that faith which, on any showing, is adequate, where it exists in its fulness, to produce and sustain the supernatural life.

But our temptation is not, I suppose, to give up a religious basis altogether, and to accept the statement that Christianity has played its part on the world's stage, and must give place to new actors. Such a temptation comes much later, when we have already left far behind the position of "steadfastness."

What, then, is the earlier phase? What is the first temptation to abandon steadfastness, to be false to our trust? "Nemo repentè venit turpissimus," and, in the same way, no one changes in a moment from faith to doubt. The transition is very gradual. Can we say where it begins? Can we say what is the first temptation to the Christian soldier to betray his trust?

We must allow, no doubt, much for imperfect education, as well as for special temptations, which will vary with the individual; but generally I think it will be true to say that he is in imminent danger of losing his steadfastness—that is, remember, of being false to his trust,—who has no clear notion as to the truths which he has to defend. And here, in fairness, I must confess that we clergy are to blame in not putting more clearly before men the outlines of that truth which we are charged to keep and hand on The consequence is that men are driven to a kind of empirical theologizing, attempting, with necessarily imperfect knowledge, to co-ordinate for themselves the truths of religion, and those which follow as consequences from them. In such a process, certain truths seem to them to be detached from the main body of Christian belief, and they become less careful about them. I am not speaking *à priori*, I have known it to be so in very many cases; men who would have shrunk from abandoning the great central truths of the Faith, were persuaded to think of certain other truths as indifferent. They could not see how these were connected with that which they would have fought for to the last, and so they gave them up; and only when it was too late did they learn that they had coolly admitted the enemy to the outworks, and now find the very citadel besieged. And then there comes a great struggle, a struggle which saddens the life and wastes the strength, a struggle carried on at grievous odds, because all unconsciously we gave the enemy his advantage. Don't be led to think that you can detach one truth from the great unity of the faith without imperilling the whole. You may not see the peril, and the consequences may not follow immediately, but follow they will and must, if in little things you can be persuaded to be false to your trust. "The Three Creeds" are not a fortuitous collection of dogmatic formularies,[1] nor are the books of the Bible a mere assemblage of ancient writings which have happened to come down to us. They are the Divine rule of Faith and Life which God has bidden us steadfastly to hold.

[1] Dr. Liddon's "Life of Faith and Athanasian Creed," p. 24.

You will see that I am thinking rather of those who are deceived into abandoning their steadfastness; and yet at the risk of saying what to some will seem unkind and hard, I must remind you that steadfastness is often lost by men by their own fault, and with their eyes open. I know there are men even amongst ourselves who have drifted away from God's truth, while they honestly thought that they were holding it fast. But I cannot but know, also, that there are those who are, and know they are, false to the trust committed to them. I can respect the rationalist who, by patient study and careful search, arrives at results which I feel to be false. I cannot and will not respect that superficial "Broad-Churchism," as it is sometimes called, which, under cover of claiming a higher intellectual position, dares to throw doubts on truths which often, perhaps, at heart it believes, or for the sake of saying some new thing, insinuates doubts about matters of faith in the home circle, or absolves itself from the trouble of understanding even the truths it assails, by speaking of them as if they belonged to an age that is gone. To my mind it is a terrible thing thus to deal with any truth; how much more, calmly to discuss, as if it were an open question, that which you will some day know to touch your very life! And yet it is often done, and at last, what is put forth as a paradox to be defended, is accepted as a fact. And then we come to speak of Divine truths as "of infinitesimally little importance," because, from first to last, we know "infinitesimally little" about them. And then others, who see the utter vagueness and uncertainty into which our so-called intellectual attitude has brought us, throw themselves into the great dogmatic system of the Roman Church, just because it is definite, and corresponds to a real want.

It is a remarkable fact of our day that when English Churchmen, some wilfully, some unconsciously, are giving up the clear and definite faith of our fathers, for fear they should offend people by sharply defined dogmatic statements, the cry of the most earnest among the Dissenting sects, the representatives, remember, of undogmatic Christianity is, We want more definiteness in our faith, more unity among ourselves, if we are to be saved from degenerating into a mere political propaganda. Our definite faith as English Churchmen is our strength. Neither Dissenter nor unbeliever thinks the better of a Churchman who has not the courage of his assured beliefs. The moment we abandon the definiteness of our professed formularies it is thrown in our teeth. Nay, it is not long since indefiniteness was charged against the Church of England as its great fault, and that by one who was himself a minister of an undogmatic Christian sect. His words are true, strange as they sound from such a source. They are true, and worth remembering. "The world has nothing to expect from a religion which reduces to a clammy, colourless pulp the great facts and truths of the Catholic Faith."

[1] Baldwin Brown.

III.

MORAL STRENGTH.

"Watch ye, stand fast in the faith, quit you like men, be strong. Let all your things be done with charity."—1 COR. xvi. 13, 14.

THE third great duty to which S. Paul exhorts the Christian soldier is *manliness*. "Quit yourselves like men (ἀνδρίζεσθε)." "Be men," and act like men in the great conflict. It is an appeal not merely to duty, but to what we call self-respect. Act worthily of yourselves, worthily of the place which you hold in God's world.

What is that place? It needed neither the revelation of the Law nor the revelation of the Gospel to teach man that he had a great place to fill in the world. The original revelation of the natural light—call it conscience or reason, or what you will—was enough to show man that he was something infinitely higher than the beasts that perish, that somehow or other, he knew not how, he was in relation with that which was around him and about him, and yet inconceivably above him. There was that which belonged to him in common with the whole animal world, but that, least of all, was his real self. His real self was that in which he was most like God, and the thought that he could in any degree approach that which was so infinitely above him was his stimulus in all high and noble action. And all through the varying phases of psychological speculation, the higher and nobler natures clung fast to that thought. We are men, not brutes, and being men, we are almost gods. Let us act worthily of such greatness; let us crush out all that will degrade us back to the mere animal, and quit ourselves like men.

But then the ancient world, apart from revelation, while it had seized the fact of man's greatness, man's dignity, had still to learn his true relation to that higher something which was called God, before man could know his true place in God's world. And so we are not surprised to find that that virtue which was highest in ancient systems, manliness (*ἀνδρεία*) was accompanied by pride and self-consciousness and contempt of others. The honour of humanity was still unknown. The ancients knew that man was great, even that he was like God; but they knew little as yet of what God was.

Turn now to the first chapter of revelation, and see the endorsing of that truth which man's consciousness had already seized, "God created man in His own image, in the image of God created He him." That added nothing, could have told man nothing, if that same volume of revelation had not gone on to unfold God's nature, His perfect holiness His awful purity, His universal Fatherhood, His infinite love, His justice, which could not clear the guilty, His mercy which would not see the sinner die except by his will, all gathered up in Him, the Divine Son, Who, while being the brightness of the Father's glory, and the express image of His person, was yet found in fashion as a man, dying (such is the utter self-sacrifice of perfect love) that men might live, taking our nature into God, that the ancient likeness which sin had marred, God Himself might outline again.

Man is in God's image, is rightly said even of those who know it not, who have never heard of God save in the restless longings of their heart after something above and beyond themselves. They are in the image of God; that is their greatness. There is something in them worthy of reverence and love, something which we may appeal to against that lower self, which is not the true self.

In what does that image of God consist? In days when people valued clearness and definiteness as something higher than mistiness and vagueness, holy men tried in the light of the Christian revelation to tell us wherein man is like God. And, in order to do this, they distinguished between three things.

I. The image of God, in which man was first made.

II. The image of God, so far as it was restored by the Incarnation, and—

III. The likeness to God, which is the end and aim of the Christian life, when by the indwelling of the Holy Spirit "Christ is formed in us," and we are conformed to the image of Christ.

For our purpose, however, it is also necessary to

point out the nature of the likeness itself. And here, again, old theological distinctions will help us.

Man is like God in that which distinguishes him from the brute creation, *in his reason and in his moral freedom.* Out and beyond this, there is still something like God, though sin has terribly marred its likeness. Yet in man's affections, in his craving for sympathy and love, in his instinctive desire to correct wrong, to avoid defilement, to return kindnesses—nay, to do kind acts without reward or thought of self—there is that which has been called the trace of God's nature, the "vestigium Dei." And so in this call to "Quit yourselves like men," I will ask you to think of it specially as an appeal to you to act *as beings possessed of reason, as endowed with moral freedom, as well as possessors of affections* which, till they are destroyed, and their nature marred by earthly things, are *of God.*

"*Quit yourselves like men.*" There was a time when it was thought enough to put aside religion with the patronizing remark that it was all very well for women and children; but men, except the clergy, who were supposed to have an interest in keeping it up, can do very well without it. And yet, as a matter of fact, we find Christianity the ruling power in some of the *strongest* men, and the source of wisdom to some of the *wisest* men, and the end and aim of some of the *greatest* men; and that, not merely accidentally, but because in them, at all events, there was a real connection between their religion and that which we admire in their lives. They would not have been what they were if they had not believed what they did believe. And it is a real help to us to find that at least, in these cases, religion is at the root of manliness; that without saying there is no manliness apart from religion, we may truly say that religion, if it is real, makes us manly.

Now, I have said that that which constitutes man's greatness, because it is that in which his likeness to God is seen, is *reason* and *moral freedom*. But we cannot separate these. Reason implies moral freedom, and moral freedom implies reason. They are gathered up into that which is of the essence of manliness, *moral strength*, the power of throwing one's whole nature into one great purpose, one irresistible effort which compels success, and triumphs over opposition.

You are called upon, as Christian soldiers, to show your manliness, your *moral strength*. "Quit yourselves like men." In the prime of life men do not need to be told to admire strength, whether it shows itself in the competitions for university or college distinctions in intellectual matters, or in those other competitions on the river, or in the cricket-field, or elsewhere. But it is useful to remind ourselves that the reason why we admire excellence in such different spheres is that both exhibit that characteristic of true manliness which we call *moral strength*. Mere animalism or mere intellectualism wins no admiration and no prize. For what we admire is the concentration of moral force upon an object—the subordination of everything in one's self which hinders us in the pursuit, the willingness "to scorn delights, and live laborious days," to deny ourselves in order to get nearer to the end, to forego many of the temptations and attractions of social intercourse that we may give ourselves more unreservedly to that which we feel to be our life work, or the preparation for it; or in the other sphere of amusement and devotion to what are rightly called manly sports, the will to submit ourselves to training, to discipline, to live by rule, the readiness to have faults corrected, to take an inferior place, and do our duty in it; above all, to crush out all that would put mere selfish gratification before the success for which all are working—all this implies something of self-discipline for a purpose; in a word, it implies *moral strength.* That is why—though our work up here is work, and not amusement—the success of the college, or the river, or the cricket-ground is full of meaning. It means that the spirit of manly self-restraint exists among us, as surely as failure in such sports indicates something at least of effeminacy and want of strength. Of course moral strength may be wrongly directed; it may be directed to what is recreation, to the detriment of that which is our work. But that is not a question which is now before us. What I want you to notice is that where-ever we see that which we call manly in any sphere, it means moral strength, the concentration of one's whole self in an effort to realize a definite end.

Now, how will this *moral strength* show itself in the Christian warfare? For we are bidden to be manly, to play the man in the struggle against sin—

mainly, in two forms, *singleness of purpose* and *decision of character*.

I. By *singleness of purpose* I mean setting before ourselves one object in life, and one only, making everything else subservient to it, drawing all our studies and all our amusements that way, making everything conduce to it, and all the parts of our nature concentrate themselves upon it. Is that possible? Only for those who think it worth a great effort to play the man. Only for those who have taken the trouble to find out what they were created for. No man is created without a definite work to do, or with more works than one, or without the power to find out what his one work, his vocation, as we call it, is. There are very many vocations, but they are but different ways of doing the work of man as man. Some are called to be priests, and to quit themselves like men in a calling which, if it be rightly exercised, will need much moral strength. Some are called to serve God as laymen—and God knows there was never greater need than there is now of men who, being laymen, are willing to live as servants of Christ. We are all, whether we will or no, soldiers fighting in a great fight; some are called to this post, some to that, some to garrison duty, some to what seems more active duty in the field. But fight we must, unless—it is the only alternative—we are traitors to our King. Is it a great thing to say that the Church to which you belong "expects every man to do his duty?" You cannot do that if you have gods many and lords many. You have only one heart, and it will be where the "one treasure" is; and your head will obey your heart, and work for that which your heart loves. You cannot serve God and Mammon, not merely because the love of the world and the love of God are opposed, but because a divided aim means the loss of moral strength. If a college is split up into cliques with different interests and different aims, if its *esprit de corps* is lost, as a college it loses strength, the power of throwing itself by an act of patriotism into some one common effort is gone. So with the individual. If he has a divided aim, his moral strength is impaired, there are factions within the city. It is only unity which can resist the enemy's attack.

Am I saying what is not almost obviously true, when I say that there are some among us, perhaps many, who are trying to live this double life? They join in our chapel services, they even sometimes draw near to the Holy Altar; but that which their thoughts turn first and naturally to, is something different. They have come up to Oxford to fit themselves for life in the world, that is to say, to acquire a competent knowledge of Latin and Greek, and if they get that, it is all they want. They leave us as they found us. They have other interests, other views of life; they go out from among us, yet they are not of us, and why? Because from first to last they have not realized the terrible struggle into which they will be plunged, —which life up here ought to have fitted them to face. You do not know yet what going out into the world means. You know there will be competitions and rivalries, and you hope to hold your own; but have you thought of that other conflict which you must face—a conflict from which, in great measure, you are here protected—a conflict with spiritual forces of evil and wickedness. How will you play the man, how will you fight the good fight, how will you be able to stand, if you will not, while here, put on your armour, train and discipline and school yourselves, gathering up all the powers of your being for one great noble effort, that, when the conflict comes, you may "quit yourselves like men?"

II. *Decision of character*, I spoke of, as the other main form in which moral strength will shew itself. Decision of character implies definiteness of knowledge, as well as strength of will. And neither of these come in a moment. We see that, in ordinary matters, it is the sudden emergency which tests a man's real strength. How will he act? Will he know what to do? and will he have the presence of mind to do it? A man of decision of character always takes the lead in critical moments. Men offer to him the homage which is always instinctively rendered to greatness. Others are wavering, discussing this expedient and that, and the really strong man is calm and collected. He seems to have an almost supernatural insight into what is the right thing to be done, and his calmness and assurance gives strength to others. How often are we called upon to show such decision of character in the spiritual warfare? and how rarely is it to be found? We stop, and hesitate, and argue *pro* and *con*, and discuss utilitarian considerations, and that which would have cut through all these in a moment—the manly decision of a formed character—is wanting just when it is called for. What does this mean, but that we have no real moral strength, no manliness; at least, we have not the courage to quit ourselves like men?

For is not the very notion of moral freedom the choosing what is right because it is right, and apart from its consequences? As children, we are swayed and influenced by the example of others, but as men, who have put away childish things, we profess to act freely. And what is the consequence? Why, again and again the story of that weak king Joash is repeated, the king who acted rightly and served God all the days of Jehoiada the priest; but the moment that kind guardianship was gone, his goodness departed like the morning cloud. It isn't really that, in the strength of our formed judgment, we reverse the instinctive judgments of childhood. It is that from mere pliancy and ductility of will, mere effeminacy and want of manliness, we take our cue from those around us. We are the slaves of public opinion, nowhere more than here in Oxford, where eccentricity is admired as originality. We haven't the pluck to stand alone. What do other men do? What is the tradition in other colleges? Of course we must do what is "the thing." And yet they who measure themselves by themselves, and compare themselves among themselves, are not wise or manly either. For strength, moral strength, often means voting with the minority, perhaps standing alone. Even amongst our own companions, we are bound, if we "quit ourselves like men," sometimes to stand alone. Have you never been in company when you felt that if you had had a little more strength you could not have sat still as you did? When the profane jest, or the indecent story, or the song bordering on lewdness made your colour rise, made you feel for a moment that you would gladly be free from such company. And looking back to that time, can you feel that you played the man, or that you lost your chance of speaking one word for God? Did you never sit through a discussion in which the whole question under debate was treated from a purely prudential and popular point of view, when you felt that if you had had the courage to speak, it was no open question, but one which, but for the want of moral strength, and the willingness of each to go with the multitude, was already settled.

There is a time to speak and a time to be silent. How shall we know when it would be mere self-assertion to protest, mere weakness to sit still? Can you give us any rule? No; but I can give you principles, which are better than rules. Practise manly decision of character where there is no doubt. Train yourself to decide at once according to the rule of right, whatever comes. Let the decisions of your conscience be final and irreversible. Never look to others for your standard when you know already what is right; then, in the moment of sudden trial, when you are called upon to decide, you will be able, come what will, to "quit yourselves like men."

IV.

DIVINE STRENGTH.

"Watch ye, stand fast in the faith, quit you like men, be strong."—
1 COR. xvi. 13.

"BE strong." It would seem, at first sight, as if only an artificial distinction could be drawn between those two injunctions, "Quit you like men," "Be strong," ἀνδρίζεσθε, κραταιοῦσθε. But, looking more closely into the meaning of the words, we find that, not only are they not synonymous, they do not even overlap. Ἀνδρίζεσθε, a word which occurs nowhere else in the New Testament, has an obvious and definite meaning. It is an appeal to self-respect, and a call to us to show forth our manliness, or, as I preferred to call it, in order to avoid some associations connected with that word, our moral strength. Κραταιοῦσθε, on the other hand, in the only three other passages in which it is used, definitely refers to a different kind of strength. Twice it is used of our Lord Himself growing strong in spirit,[1] ἐκραταιοῦτο πνεύματι, and once it is used by S. Paul in the Epistle to the Ephesians,[2] in the phrase, "strengthened with might

[1] S. Luke i. 80; ii. 40.

[2] Eph. iii. 16.

by His Spirit in the inner man." The word thus becomes almost synonymous with another favourite word of S. Paul's, ἐνδυναμοῦσθαι, constantly translated by the English, "strengthened," or made strong, and always with reference to Divine strength. Be strong in the Lord, and in the power of His might.[1] Be strong in the grace that is in Christ Jesus.[2] It refers definitely to that strength which made S. Paul himself strong for his work,[3] even as spiritual heroes in all ages, "out of weakness were made strong."[4]

We are bidden to play the man, to act worthily of all that is highest and best in ourselves, to throw ourselves on our higher self, and "Quit us like men." But in our struggles here this is not enough. For we are wrestling not against flesh and blood, but against the leagued forces of a supernatural power, against "spiritual wickedness in high places," and if we are to fight not only manfully, but victoriously, we must meet the supernatural by the supernatural. And that we may fight victoriously, God in His goodness has so ordered it, that, as the spiritual life advances, this higher self is lost and swallowed up in something higher than itself. Our higher self, that which makes us men, not brutes, is the image of God in which we were created, the image which Christ came to renew, and this, by the supernatural power of the Holy Spirit, is drawn into likeness and union with Him to Whom we were likened at the first. Our strength is thus not merely *moral* strength,

[1] Eph. vi. 10. [2] 2 Tim. ii. 1. [3] Phil. iv. 13; 1 Tim. i. 12.
[4] Heb. xi. 34.

it is *spiritual* and *divine,* and "the weapons of our warfare are not carnal, but mighty through God to the pulling down of strongholds." So convinced was S. Paul of the absolute necessity of this supernatural strength for the Christian soldier that he often speaks of all other strength as if it were only weakness, and of no value in the great conflict. But it is easy to misunderstand S. Paul's language, and it has been misunderstood to mean that there is no such thing as human or moral strength to which we may appeal in the great struggle with evil. Of the many false systems of doctrine invented in the sixteenth century, there is one which has sunk deep into the consciousness of English Christianity, and is now working itself out to the bitter end, alienating from the truth men of high and noble character by its false teaching as to the nature of God and man. According to this teaching, the Divine image is not only marred, but utterly destroyed by the fall.[1] We have not even moral freedom, or high aspirations, or natural yearnings for the holy and the pure. "Man," we are told, "has been so banished from the kingdom of God, that all in him which bears reference to the blessed life of the soul is extinct."[2] In place of the image of God, there is nothing but "horrible deformity."[3] Calvin is not indeed always consistent on this matter; but this is the view which has left its mark on the popular preaching of the English Church. It has not indeed followed him in his terrible doctrine

[1] Cf. Moehler, Instit., iii. c. 2, n. 12. [2] Instit., ii. c. 2. n. 22.
[3] i. c. 15, p. 71.

that all that was good and noble in the heathen world was due to the fact that God gave the heathen "some taste of His own Divinity," (they are Calvin's words, not mine), in order that they might be condemned, as it were, out of their own mouth.[1] If a man can believe that, we are prepared for a teaching about God wholly irreconcilable with the revelation that "God is love."

It has been necessary for me to allude to this false teaching, because I have ventured to speak of moral strength or natural strength as a fact in our nature, to be found in man as man, heathen as well as Christian; because in man as man, there is still the image of God, marred in all by the fact of sin, sketched anew in all when human nature was taken into God, though it can be brought into perfect likeness with God only by that supernatural life which implies union with God Himself. In the perfect life, the human and the Divine strength will be seen working together; the human transformed and transfigured, but not destroyed, by that which is called Divine. And yet in their origin, both are Divine. Of both, it is true to say that "So great is the goodness of the Lord towards all men that He considers His own gifts as their merits." [2] Moral strength is His gift as much as that other strength which we call supernatural. The one comes in and through our nature, the other is from without, a special gift of God. We may see the difference in that well-known story which we

[1] See Moehler, p. 72.
[2] Council of Trent, ap. Moehler, 154.

read as our first lesson to-night.[1] A great temptation was met by a noble resistance. Such a resistance might, no doubt, have been made by a heathen, in virtue of his moral strength. The natural sense of justice, strengthened by a no less natural feeling of gratitude to his master, might have enabled Joseph to resist. Indeed, these natural feelings came first in the chronological order, even in Joseph's mind. His master's trust in him, how could he be false to that? His master's kindness. "He hath kept back nothing from me but thee, because thou art his wife;" and then in a moment the supernatural power of one who was in conscious union with God appeared. "How can I do this great wickedness, and sin against God?" The other arguments might have been met and overcome. For the heart is deceitful and ready to justify sin, and in the face of that temptation, especially, mere human strength so often fails. But that other argument admitted of no discussion. "How can I do this great wickedness, and sin against God?" And so his higher self, which, even apart from conscious union with God, would have called him to resist manfully, was taken up into something higher still by the consciousness of a definite relationship with God.

There are no good acts done without the grace of God, for, separated from Christ, we can do nothing; but men often think they are standing alone, because as yet He has not revealed Himself to them. Really God deals with men as a father does with a little child. "Walk a little by my hand," He seems to

[1] Genesis xxxix.

say, "and then I will carry you. Act up to what is noblest and best in you, and I will give you something higher still." "Quit you like men," and you shall "be strong" in a strength which is Divine.

What is that Divine strength which is to transform our natural and human strength? In one word, it is "Christ in us," the same Divine power which secretly fought in and with the noblest efforts of humanity outside the Jewish and the Christian Church. Only now its nature is revealed; more than that, there is revealed to us the means by which that Divine strength may be gained—the channels of communication have been thrown open to us. The end and aim of the religious life has been made clear—likeness to God, Christ formed in us, ourselves transformed, our lower self subdued, our higher self taken into God. "I live, yet not I, but Christ liveth in me." "In all these things we are more than conquerors through Him that loved us." So speaks S. Paul.

This is the great sacramental truth of the Christian Revelation, and by its sacramental teaching, Christianity must stand or fall. For it is in this that Christianity is perfectly distinguished from all other religions. That is why the sacramental teaching of Christianity is always the first attacked. For if that can be disposed of, Christianity differs only in degree from other religious systems. It only fills in more definitely and clearly the content of the Moral Law. It only tells us more precisely which is the perfection which we have been unconsciously reaching out for. And if we are willing to go so far as to say that the perfect man of the Gospels was not an imagination of the Evangelists, but a real historical person; nay, if we go so far as to allow that He was God as well as man, that admission without its corollary—the sacramental teaching of Christianity, as I have called it—takes away from the perfection of the ideal. For Jesus Christ is then taken out of the roll of common men. It is no model for us—only a far-off vision of beauty, seen for a moment and then withdrawn; something which we cannot hope to realize, and the less earnest natures will settle down as before, into contented mediocrity; and those who are more earnest will be saddened and disappointed. It is so beautiful, but so far off. It cannot help us. As well may we hope—

> "to hold a fire in our hand,
> By thinking on the frosty Caucasus;
> Or cloy the hungry edge of appetite,
> By bare imagination of a feast;
> Or wallow naked in December's snows,
> By thinking on fantastic summer's heat."

The image only mocks us by its moral perfectness. And it is cruel, cruel to set before us such a model, only to bring home to us our own inability to realize it.

But in what I have called the sacramental teaching of Christianity, its strength lies, and by that it must be judged. Modern systems which take from Christianity only its moral ideal, seem to me like those false exorcists in the Acts, who took upon themselves to assail evil spirits with, "We adjure you by Jesus, Whom Paul preacheth." The powers of evil are not vanquished thus. They know their strength and their weakness. "Jesus I know, and Paul I know, but who are ye?" Christ's word is with power. By that same power His Apostles spoke; by that same power His Church speaks still. "Be strong." It was the same in the spiritual as in the physical sphere. "Take up thy bed and walk," and lo! the palsied limbs grew strong. "His word was with power." In the spiritual sphere we are bidden to be strong, to stand; and He Who by His Apostle gives the command, gives us the power to obey it. This is the sacramental truth of the Christian religion. It does not set before us simply a model to be imitated. He Who is Himself the pattern of perfect humanity has made it possible for us to be like Him, and all that we call the means of grace are but the different helps which He has given us, enabling us to be like Him, nay, one with Him, in a mystical union. And in Holy Baptism, the gate of the Sacraments, we are born again to newness of life in Him. We die with Him, for death is the penalty of sin, that we may live the risen life with Him. And in Holy Communion, that other Sacrament which is necessary—necessary, that is, for all, we are one with Christ, and Christ with us; one, that is, with the Conqueror of death and sin, and therefore sharing in His victory. But those two necessary Sacraments do not cover the whole field of our relations with God. There is Prayer, which has been called "suppliant omnipotence," by which we throw ourselves into the arms of God, and recognize the truth that the conflicts with which we are engaged is His rather than ours. There is the devotional study of God's Word, by which a new source of strength is opened to us as God reveals Himself to us in it. There is that great spiritual society, the Church, into which Baptism admits us, bringing us, as it were, within the sphere of the operations of sacramental grace. There is that means of grace, call it Sacrament or not, as you will, in which we recognize specially the ministry of reconciliation. Confession and Absolution, not indeed necessary for all, but infinitely more necessary, surely, than people think for those who would be strong in assured union with God.

How many of us are using to the full these sources of Divine strength? To some extent, we all use them. We do not discard prayer, public or private, or Bible reading, though it is to be feared we reduce them to a minimum. Nor do we altogether neglect Holy Communion. Only, if one may judge by the numbers of those who communicate, there must be many who have not yet realized the truth that Communion is a real source of Divine strength, strength for the battle of life, strength which is to make us *manly*. There is nothing manly in neglecting that which gives us strength. We don't think a man wise because he refuses to learn from those who can give him knowledge, nor do we think it a proof of moral strength to neglect those means which God has provided to make us strong.

If I may speak quite freely, and for myself alone, I think, in this college of ours, we want to see more of the conscious appeal to Divine and superhuman strength. Moral strength there is, and we are thankful for it, but we want to see those who are most strong in what we call moral strength, openly resting it upon that which is Divine. There are some of you who, by your seniority, or your intellectual position, are, whether you will or no, looked up to by the rest of the society. You are like the elder brothers in the family. You are making the traditions by which the next generation will live. And you are setting, I believe, a good example of moral strength, of self-denying effort in that which is your special work up here. You are ready to frown down at once those tendencies which, if they are developed in such a socicty, sap the strength of the whole community.

Well, the ideal of college life is, that those who arc strongest in the strength which is human and natural, should not be afraid to seek the strength which is from God. You are, by the circumstances of your studies perhaps, exposed to dangers which others may not know. That is a reason, surely, for throwing yourselves more often than others on the strength which is Divine. Yet hard reading is made an excuse for irregularity in chapel services, just as in ordinary life the distractions of business are alleged in excuse for Sunday idleness. Yet, if Christianity offers *strength*, as it does, if you are called to communion with God just that you may be strong for your daily work, all the arguments tend the other way. And that is the way they must tend, if we believe Christianity is a religion which gives strength. And I would commend this thought specially to two classes of men, who, it seems to me, are specially exposed to danger, and therefore need special strength; first, those who are studying Philosophy, and next, those who are giving themselves to Theology. The former class are brought face to face with the greatest problems of life. They are bound to know what are the human and natural explanations of these which have been attempted, and they need strength—strength of character and strength of will—if they are to stand fast in the faith. The others are in special danger from mere familiarity with sacred things. I do not think I am saying what many will not bear me out in, when I say that reading Theology for the schools, writing essays on the great mysteries of the Faith, discussing the bearing of various heresies on the great central truth of Christ's Divinity, is a constant source of danger and unreality. If those who are reading Theology are not led to feel more and more their need of Divine strength, if they are beginning to get careless about their Communions, as is often the case, they ought to ask themselves very anxiously whether their studies in Theology are not being made the devil's means of drawing them away from God.

One objection, and one only, I will touch upon, because it is so very plausible, so very false. It is sometimes said, You tell us to be manly, and yet you bid us subject ourselves to a higher power working in us. Religious people are so weak. They have no self-reliance. They are but feeble creatures, after all, with all their boasted strength. How can you expect men to set before themselves, as an end, what, disguise it as you will, is self-surrender, which means renouncing all that we admire as manly in us. I will answer by some negative instances sufficient, at all events, to prove that surrendering one's self to the will of God, resting on His strength, is a source not of weakness but of power. Was S. Paul feeble and nerveless because his will was surrendered to the will of Christ? Did he speak less powerfully, or run less certainly, or fight as "one that beateth the air," because he had learned to say, "Not I, but Christ in me"? Are enthusiasts of all ages and all creeds, fanatics, if you will, wanting in force and energy, because they believe themselves to be only passive instruments in the hands of some mightier power?

And what about ourselves? Do we walk the less firmly through the darkness, because our eye is fixed upon a Light that never flickers, never is obscured, because we have ceased to follow those wandering fires which are but the exhalations from the swamp of self-love and self-indulgence and self-gratification? No; we all know something of the meaning of the paradox, "When I am weak, then am I strong." Goliath, with his sword and his spear and his shield, was no match for the stripling who met him "in the Name of the Lord of hosts, the God of the armies of Israel." It is the surrender of self to Him Who "saveth not with sword or spear," which gives real strength. "Without Him we can do nothing," but we can do all things through Christ Which strengtheneth us. It is this which has made the weak valiant, and nerved the arm of those who fought nobly for the truth. This is the strength which shows itself in great endurance, which, in olden days, made even the weakness of women strong to face the fires of martyrdom. In quietness and confidence they could dare to wait for the victory. For the battle they were fighting was the battle of the Lord, and the strength in which they fought was the strength of Him Who is stronger than the strong. "Not my will, but Thine, O Lord," is the watchword. Thy enemies are my enemies, Thy friends my friends. In Thy victory I am more than conqueror; in the triumph of Thy kingdom is my exceeding great reward.

V.

CHARITY IN ALL THINGS.

"Let all your things be done with charity."—I COR. xvi. 14.

TO-DAY[1] is "Mothering Sunday," the day on which, according to an old English tradition which survives in many parts of the country, the central thought is "home" and "family affection," when the grown-up sons and daughters gather in the old home—the earthly type of that Jerusalem which is above, the mother of us all. And not only the Epistle is appealed to, but the Gospel and the Lesson are thought to carry on the same idea; the story of Joseph entertaining his brethren, as well as the feeding of the five thousand in the Gospel, are more or less fancifully worked into the commemoration. But if the earthly home is a symbol of heaven, the home of all God's family, surely the parable of the feeding of the five thousand gives us a new meaning to "family affection." There were the multitudes gathered round, hungry, and ready to faint, and to feed them there was nothing but the five barley loaves and two small fishes—barely enough for the little family, the Lord

[1] The Fourth Sunday in Lent.

and His chosen disciples. What were they among so many? Nothing in themselves, but, distributed in obedience to Divine command, enough for all, enough and to spare. Even so, natural affection, like natural strength, is taken up into something higher than itself. It is not destroyed, but transformed. Moral strength becomes the organ by which Christ's Spirit works, and lo! it is omnipotence. "I can do all things through Christ Which strengtheneth me." And family affection has a new meaning read into it. It is world-wide, all-embracing—in a word, it is Christian love or charity, knowing no limits but those of the one family in heaven and earth, the children of the One Father.

"Let all your things be done with charity." Such is the injunction with which our Lenten Addresses close; and coming as this command does at the end of S. Paul's Epistle, and following immediately on those several duties of Watchfulness, Steadfastness, Manliness, and Strength, there was surely a reference back to that wonderful thirteenth chapter, in which he had spoken of charity in all its varied characteristics. Remember, he seems to say, that without charity these things "are nothing worth." Your duties to God, without love, become mere religiousness; your good deeds to men are unreal too, unless they, too, are the work of love. But it is obviously impossible, within the limits of a sermon, to speak of love showing itself in all those duties on which we have been insisting. And, therefore, I shall begin by limiting our subject, and speaking specially of love in reference to one of those duties, which, it is sometimes assumed, is inconsistent with true charity in the sense of love to man. I mean, of course, the duty of steadfastness and definiteness in the Faith. It is often assumed that definite faith is opposed to toleration, and that Christian love is opposed to definiteness. Now, both assumptions are false. What is the truth? Definiteness and toleration are neither necessarily connected nor necessarily opposed. It is possible to hold fast "the faith once delivered to the saints," and yet to be wanting in gentleness and considerateness, and some toleration towards those who do not hold the truth. On the other hand, real kindness and sympathy, and Christ-like love for others are to be found (who will deny it?) in those who believe most definitely in our Creed.

But of these two alternatives, the last is normal, the first abnormal. The last is what God intended, and His disciples enjoined; the first is the frustrating of His Will through human narrowness and littleness. In God's purpose, surely toleration is the *counterpart*, not the *antithesis*, of definite faith. The two belong to one another, though men often separate them. We are to "hold fast the form of sound words" in faith and love—in *faith*, which must be definite if it is *real*, in *love*, which must be tolerant if toleration is a virtue. Toleration, in fact, if we understand it rightly, is nothing but Christian charity in the presence of error.

But here we are met by a difficulty. This Christian charity, which ought to go with definite faith, is parodied by a state of feeling which "is of the earth, earthy." There is a sham toleration to which I have alluded before, which at first sight has much in common with Christian love, and which, nevertheless, is simply the negative of charity. The devil is a wonderful copyist. The tares are strangely like the wheat, and it needs a practised eye to enable a man to say, "An enemy hath done this."

Now, this toleration, which is commonly glorified as the virtue of the day—the common virtue of good, ordinary men, unless they happen to be hampered by a definite creed—what does it mean? It means we shall be told to "live and let live," to have our own opinions, and let others have theirs—not to persecute one who disagrees with us, either with the old-fashioned weapons of fire and sword, or the more modern weapons of social or political disabilities. We must not lay claim to infallibility for our views; we must allow the possibility that others may be right, and we may be wrong. What can sound more Christian than all this? The tares are strangely like the wheat, even when they are growing side by side.

Looking, however, more closely into the matter, we find that this "live-and-let-live" theory, in some circumstances, necessarily disappears, because to maintain it would be positively uncharitable. And we find that that which more than anything else modifies this Christian-like toleration is the possession of *truth*. Opposing theories, however probable, must be tolerant, for either or neither may eventually be established; but the opposite of truth is error. If, then, toleration means the readiness to believe that either of two rival positions may be true, or that both may be ultimately proved false, it is clear that *truth*, by its very nature, is *intolerant* in this sense. More than that, if the truth be one of vital importance to man in his daily life, it will become, in the hands of charity and love, not only intolerant but *aggressive.* To apply a "live-and-let-live" theory in such a case is, in fact, to justify a theory of "*live and let die.*" If such truths as we believe, truths of such awful, practical import, are not true, if they are a mere theory as to an unsolved and insoluble problem, then we are narrow-minded, and bigoted, and unchristian, to attempt to force them upon others. But if they are what we believe them to be, a revelation from God for the salvation of men, charity compels us to declare them unshrinkingly. In contending earnestly and definitely for the "faith once delivered to the saints," we are but fulfilling the first duty of brotherly love. In a book which appeared some years ago, I remember being struck by a remarkable admission. After the teaching of Jesus of Nazareth had been patronizingly commended for its high morality, and then condemned for what was called its narrowness and intolerance, the author went on to say (I quote from memory), "Of course, if what Jesus said of Himself had been true, this intolerance would have been the truest charity."

"If it had been true." Truth must be intolerant of error. In the collision of human systems, charity demands unlimited toleration. When the Gospel of Jesus Christ is revealed, there is no ἄλλο εὐαγγέλιον which is not ἕτερον εὐαγγέλιον, and we want men, in the strength of love and charity, to have the courage to say so. For a practical rule of conduct, we can hardly get beyond that grand maxim. "In necessariis unitas, in dubiis libertas, in omnibus caritas." Only do not follow the fashion of our age in confusing the different spheres of the necessary and the doubtful, the permanent and the transient—that which is one and the same for all, and that which varies indefinitely in different churches, and different places, and different times. There are many who are anxious to set Liberty against Unity, and in the end to destroy Charity.

"Stand fast in the faith," and "let all your things be done in charity." Be tolerant still. Make every allowance that the charity, which hopeth all things, can suggest,—allowance for individual character, for family surroundings, for imperfect education. Do not assume bad motives to account for forms of belief or practice, which, judged by the standard of Christian truth, you know to be false. Do not take it for granted that every founder of a sect is a Diotrephes, or that every schismatic takes a wicked pleasure in rending the robe of Christ. Christian charity requires that you should assume conscientiousness in those who differ from you. Only do not forget that conscientiousness is often as far removed from truth, as "honest doubt" from faith. Never allow yourself to be blinded as to the strict line of demarcation between true and false. Never allow yourselves to settle down into a quiescent and satisfied state, as if though Christianity may be true for you, something else may be right for another. This is no toleration, but a lack of charity. It is a position impossible for those who believe definitely that their creed is true, and are also fired with love for their brethren. For if I believe, as I do believe, that for a baptized Christian to abandon any part of his Christianity, or to invent something he likes better, or to leave out of sight what he does not approve, or to adopt something which he thinks simpler than what God has revealed, is a dangerous thing; if I believe, as I do believe, that he is imperilling his own eternal salvation, that his spiritual state is far more critical than that of the heathen who never knew Christ;—then, the more I love him, the more earnestly I shall warn him of his danger. Intolerant that may be, but it is neither unkind nor uncharitable. It is as inhuman as it is unchristian, to see a man walking blindfold into danger without an attempt to save him, just because every man has a right to go which way he will, and I am not bound to interfere. *Interfere I must.* It is only the spirit of the world which will say that I was wrong, that I was not my brother's keeper. That is only the dictum of formulated selfishness. Christianity speaks far otherwise. "Let all your things be done in charity."

This love for man, real love, which will submit to be misunderstood, which will sacrifice itself for another, is that by which all truth in practical matters is measured. Tell the unbeliever that God has revealed Himself to His Church, and he retorts, "Then show me that all your things are done in charity, show me that the Church is full of love, for God is love." Or he takes up S. Paul's words against us: "If there is among you envying and strife, are ye not carnal, and walk as men?" Yes; the world generally may be strangely ignorant of doctrinal and theological truths, but it has a marvellous keen sight in discerning the divinity of love. Ours is a time of sharp and hostile criticism of all that lays claim to the title of religion; above all, of that which boasts a special revelation from God. And it seems as if a time of fiercer trial was to come. Already the forces of unbelievers are gathering for the fight. There is "free thought," which means random speculation, much criticizing, and little criticism. There is a looseness and laxness of morals in society which is prejudicing the great questions of Christianity. There is that sham toleration, of which I have spoken, which is a grand name for indifference, though it likes to be thought an off-shoot of Christian love, and these are making overtures to one another, alien as they are, that, like Pilate and Herod, they may combine against the truth of God.

But there is a power, an omnipotent power, to which one and all bow, a power which should be the rightful heritage of the Church of Christ. In presence of that power, criticism is disarmed, cut through, like the subtle questionings of Priest and Pharisee, by the simple truths of fact. "Whether He be a sinner or no, I know not. One thing I know, that, whereas

I was blind, now I see." Whether the Christian mysteries are true, and such as occasion demands or justifies, I know not. One thing I know. If the Christian verities are the groundwork and the basis of the Christ-like life, the life of Love, they are of God. In the presence of that Love, sham toleration owns itself to be a sham, and immorality, the lowest, basest-born child of selfishness, flies from the presence of self-sacrifice. I say that to Love one and all of the enemies of Christ must bow, and love is, and should be, the rightful heritage of the Church; for he who is a follower of God must walk in love as Christ also loved us.

And as outside the great body of professing Christians all yield to the omnipotence of love, so, within that body, the questions at issue will, as a matter of fact, be decided by an appeal to the self-same power. Where love is there is Christ; where self-sacrifice, self-forgetfulness, humility are, there I see His likeness—the outline of God Incarnate. And the Church of Christ is the Church of love,—world-wide, self-forgetting, lowly love, that love which is divine.

God forbid that we should think lightly of our glorious heritage in that pure branch of God's Holy Church to which we belong, or that we should work less earnestly, or pray less fervently, that we may show forth in it the loving life of Christ. But the end of the divisions of Christendom—and an end there must be, for God is true,—the end of our divisions will be found in the pre-eminence of love. The

Church that loves most, most universally, most unselfishly, is the Church which must triumph in the end, and win over its rivals to itself. Call it by what name you will, it stands confessed and honoured as the Church which is most Christ-like, the Church that is truly Catholic.

We are challenged by the world to justify our claim to be followers of God by a life of Christ-like love. More than that, our Lord Himself has charged on us that New Commandment, that we love one another as He has loved us; and His faithful follower, S. Paul, does but hand on the Sacred Precept when he bids the Ephesians to walk in love as Christ has loved us, or closes his injunctions to the Corinthian converts with the words, "Let all your things be done in charity."

Is such love possible? Yes; but not without much that many who profess and call themselves Christians never take into their reckonings. It is possible, but only by a life of constant self-denial. Do not misunderstand me. Self-denial, in its narrow and more moral sense will do much for us, and Lent is appointed to help us to attain the great end of love. But the life of love must be a constant self-denial, a constant warfare with prejudice, and partisanship, and sectarianism, and all that separates. It must follow us into all the little details of life, making us broad in our sympathies, meek and patient under affront and worry, kindly towards enemies, tender towards the sinful, never shrinking from the clear and definite statement of a truth, even though our motives may be misunderstood, nor from a false view of toleration letting a brother destroy himself.

"Let all your things be done in charity," and you will be carrying on the very work for which God became man; nay, you will be working in that power which is omnipotence, for God is Love.

II.

COURSE OF FIVE SERMONS

PREACHED AT ST. PAUL'S CATHEDRAL, IN LENT, 1886

ON

SOME ASPECTS OF SIN

I.

SIN AS SEPARATION FROM GOD.

"Your iniquities have separated between you and your God, and your sins have hid His face from you, that He will not hear."—ISA. lix. 2.

THE one dark, insoluble mystery of human life is SIN. It is so impossible for us to explain it; so futile to try and explain it away. It is so terribly familiar, so utterly unintelligible. It is *within* us and *around* us; it is about our path and about our bed. It is there *behind* us; we can trace it like a dark stain through the history of nations, or of our own individual lives. It is *before* us, and we see it, checking all our hopeful theories as to the advancement of the race; breaking in cruelly and inevitably on all our views of what life is or may become. It is *above* us, shutting out from us, like a dark cloud, the face of God, in Whose light alone we live. Sickness, suffering, pain, and death,—these, too, are mysteries which puzzle us, and disquiet us, and raise in us anxious questionings. But SIN baffles us. God is Love. In love He created man. In man's love, God would have rejoiced; in God's love, man would have been blessed.

And man, made in God's image, refused God, refused his own true good. He sought a separate life, and found it death. This is SIN. It is impossible; but it is true.

SIN is the unutterable mystery of our lives. And yet as the shadows of Lent deepen round us, and the Cross is seen beyond, we turn back once again—here, in the Presence of our God—to the familiar mystery, that in the light which streams from Calvary we may learn something of its meaning.

We cannot fathom the mystery of SIN; we may not even ask the questions, How? and Why? But we may contemplate the terrible fact, and remind ourselves of what it is.

For the aspect of SIN which is most obvious to us, most present to our consciousness, is not the truest view that we can gain. We confuse SIN with its consequence, and mistake the symptoms for the disease. We feel the tyranny of evil habit, we feel our helplessness and the struggle for holiness, we feel the great burden of the past upon us, we see a far-off beautiful ideal we cannot reach, we know the disorder, the dislocation, the confusion of our nature. Surely, we say, SIN is slavery, it is the disease of our nature, it is guilt, it is a wretched, endless, hopeless struggle, and the fearful looking for of a righteous judgment. No! SIN involves all these; but in itself it is something different. We can explain all these in the light of one central truth. All SIN, in its degree, *separates* the soul from God: and whatever *separates* from God is SIN.

That is the central fact about SIN. Let us keep it constantly before us. For it is there, if anywhere, that we shall find the answer to those difficulties which trouble us most; there, and there only, that we shall understand the love of the Atonement, and the meaning of the work of Christ. Other views of SIN may, indeed, bring out different sides of the truth; but there is none of those other views which may not be pressed into a false and immoral theory. But when we are startled and puzzled by questions which seem to traverse our belief in the love and justice of our God, when we are asked, How can a God of love keep His anger for ever? or when men meet us with the well-known verbal juggle, How can a finite being merit infinite punishment? then our only hope is to go back to the thought of sin as separation from God. Anger, punishment, satisfaction, debt, bondage,—these are human and earthly analogies, sanctioned indeed by Holy Scripture, but misleading and false, if they obscure the truth that GOD IS LOVE.

All SIN in its degree separates the soul from God, "and sin, when it is perfected, bringeth forth DEATH." For as the separation of the body from the soul is the death of the body, so the utter separation of the soul from God is the death of the soul. If ever it is possible for the soul, even for one moment, to be wholly separated from God, that separation is for ever. *Absolute separation from God must be eternal death.* Every hope of restoration, every prayer for pardon, every upward glance to God as the soul's true good, is based on, and is the proof of, the fact that the soul is not yet altogether separated from God. The image of God is cruelly marred, but not utterly destroyed. The trace of God's likeness is yet visible to Him. When sin drove Adam and Eve from the garden, they were yet within the limits of God's love. Their thoughts turned back to the Paradise they had lost, reached forward to the Promised Seed. This could not have been if human nature had been ruined by the Fall. Absolute ruin must have been absolute separation from God, which is eternal death.

That truth we may apply also to ourselves. Men trouble themselves with the question, Have I committed the unpardonable sin—the sin against the Holy Ghost, which has never forgiveness? Surely the answer is at hand. Nothing short of absolute separation from God precludes hope. And the soul that is absolutely severed from Him does not long for Him, or fear the separation from Him.

Sin is the great separation of the soul from Him Who is our Life. We talk of degrees of sin, of little sins and great ones, of sins mortal and sins venial. And though there is a sense in which all sins are mortal and all sins are venial, yet the distinction is a real one. Some sins tend more directly than others to widen the breach between the soul and God. We call them *mortal* because they have more power to weaken the will, and to blind the conscience; or because they imply a greater rejection of God's love, or estrange us more entirely from holy things, or bow us down more closely to the earth. And yet the little sins play a more terrible part than we know in the soul's tragedy. A great sin often brings its own visible punishment, its own recoil. We see its loathsomeness. But the little sins are so little, we hardly notice them. They are like the drizzling rain which wets us through before we think of taking shelter. The trifling acts of pride or sloth; the unchecked love of self, the evil thoughts, the word of shame, the little neglect of prayer,—ah! we never thought that these could kill down the soul, and separate from God And suddenly we awake to find that God has, as it were, dropped out of our lives. We were living the world's life, and thinking the world's thoughts, and adopting the world's standards. We never committed any great sin; we knew, indeed, that God was not in all our thoughts, and now He seems to have left us altogether, and we lift up that bitter cry of the soul in separation, "O God, cast us not away from Thy presence!"

Did God ever cast away a soul? All through my life of sinning, did God ever repel me? Did He separate me from Himself, He Who is very Love? It cannot be. "Your iniquities have separated between you and your God, and your sins have hid His face from you, that He will not hear."

And as sin is primarily the act by which the soul turns away from God, so the revelation of God's Love in Christ is primarily a *Reconciliation*, an Atonement; in the old sense of that word, an At-one-ment. Christ healed us, paid our debt, bought us with a price, satisfied the Law—all that He did; but they were all parts of the work of *reconciliation.* And that reconciliation is always in the Bible, *a reconciliation of man to God.* All the blessed means of grace which He has won for us are the modes by which He would win us back. In the Church, the Priesthood, the Sacraments, it is Christ Himself Who speaks to us, "Be ye reconciled unto God." In the Incarnation, the restoration of human nature is begun. On Calvary the work of Atonement is complete.

"God so loved the world." It was no partial thing. For God will have all men to be saved. He wills not that any should perish. Are there any who resist His Will, and reject that Reconciliation? Impossible; but it is true. God in creation willed that man should serve Him with a willing love, and man refused. God wills that all should be reconciled to Him in Christ, and men reject His love.

Sin is the unutterable mystery of our lives. We cannot solve it; but this we know—it is man's work, not God's. There is no death of a soul, but the death of suicide. "God," it has been said,[1] "will part with no one who does not say to Him, face to face, 'I will not have Thee.'" Not one soul shall be separated from Heaven which has not rejected the appeal of love: "Ye will not come unto Me, that ye might have life."

[1] Faber, ap. Pusey's letter to D. M.

II.

SIN AS DISEASE.

"Heal my soul; for I have sinned against Thee."—Ps. xli. 4.

EVERY sin, in its degree, separates from God. This is the unvarying note of sin. But separation from God, even a partial separation, or estrangement, has an immediate reflex action upon man. To turn from God is not only to reject His love, it is by that very rejection to degrade human nature. Hence the first act of sin is rightly called a *fall*, and the expulsion from Eden was the symbol of that change which sin had wrought in man.

What was that change? Theologians tell us that, by the Fall, man lost that supernatural gift whereby alone his communion with God, and a blessed immortality, were secured; and not only so, but his natural powers for good were terribly marred. And if such a sharp dividing-line between the natural and the supernatural does not commend itself to our ways of thinking, yet it is one of the most universally recognized facts of human nature, that man knows himself as a being not only estranged from God, but at strife with himself. Heathen poet and philosopher, no less than Jewish and Christian teachers, are constantly reminding us of the struggle or dualism in man's nature. "The flesh lusteth against the spirit, and the spirit against the flesh, and these are contrary the one to the other." Reason and passion, or the desires and the will, are at deadly feud. The soul of man, says Plato, is in a state of struggle, in which the beast seeks to overcome the God in man, in which the lower rises up against the higher, and destroys the harmony of the whole.[1] There is in man, says Aristotle, something which wars and strives against reason. Like a paralyzed limb, we try to move it one way, and we fail. The well-known words of a Roman poet have almost passed into a proverb: "I see the better, I pursue the worse."

But the view of sin, as the disorganization and confusion of human nature, is most common in Greek writers, both heathen and Christian, and not unfrequently, even among the heathen, it is treated as a thing which is not natural[2] to man. It is not the confusion of a chaos not yet reduced to order, but the wreck and ruin of a once fair and perfect harmony. How that confusion was produced, what was the disturbing force, they cannot tell us. Sometimes it is vaguely ascribed to pleasure, sometimes to the fact that human nature is not a simple, but a compound whole. Sometimes a Manichean view of matter, as the home of moral evil, is appealed to to explain this fact. But the fact is recognized. Man's nature is at

[1] Plato, "Rep.," ix. p. 589, ii. 365.

[2] Cf. Wordsworth's "Bampton Lectures," pp. 153, 154.

discord with itself, and it cannot have been always so It is easier to believe in two co-eternal antagonistic powers than to suppose that God made man as he is.

Sin, as the disease, the disorder of our natures—how common, and how natural is the thought in Old Testament Scriptures! In the Psalms of David, so close is the association of the disease of the body and of the soul, that we cannot mark the transition from the one to the other. All through the earlier history of the Jews, sickness and sin had been associated as effect and cause; God had taught them by that association the real kinship which we know exists between the two. And disease had come to be the natural analogue of sin, the visible symbol of the invisible, till they came to look forward to their Messiah as a Great Physician of souls, a Sun of Righteousness which should arise with healing in His wings. And when the Christ came, He gave His *imprimatur* to that association of ideas. He healed every sickness and every disease among the people; but His mission was to heal the broken-hearted, to seek and to save the lost.

It is this view of sin, as the disease and disfigurement of human nature, that is so familiar to us in the writings of S. Athanasius. "God gave us freely," he says, "by the grace of the Word, a life in correspondence with God. But men, having rejected things eternal, and, by counsel of the devil, turned to the things of corruption, became the cause of their own corruption." The image of God in man was marred yet that which had once borne the impress of God was precious in His sight. "Wherefore the Word of God came in, in His own Person, that as He was the Image of the Father, He might be able to create afresh the man after His likeness."[1]

Here the prominent thought of sin is of that which destroys the perfection of human nature, and Christ's work is a work of renewal. And so we are carried on a step. Sin is separation from God; the work of Christ is *Reconciliation.* But the turning from God has already marred the image of God in man. Reconciliation, to be perfect, must be restoration too. The nature which is no longer in perfect correspondence with God, reflecting His glory as in a mirror, is diseased, defiled, defaced. Its perfect symmetry is lost. Its harmony with itself is gone. The nature which is handed on from father to son bears an hereditary taint, the germ of a disease which, if it develop, will bring death. "Death," says S. Athanasius, "had gained a hold on man; corruption was abiding in him; the whole race was perishing. God's handiwork was in process of dissolution."

When, then, we think of that first consequence of sin, the corruption of human nature, we think of Christ's work as a work of regeneration and renewal. It is the answer to that cry, "Heal my soul; for I have sinned against Thee." He, the Saviour of the world, must heal not only the breach between God and man, but the sickness of human nature itself. And this He does by implanting in man, through union with His own perfect nature, a supernatural

[1] "De Incar.," xiii.

principle of regeneration; a germ of new life which may destroy the cause of corruption, and arrest its progress, and make human nature again capable of union with God. And this regeneration is sometimes spoken of as a momentary thing, sometimes as a progressive process. For it is not in a moment that chaos is reduced to order, or the diseased restored to health. The corrupt nature struggles still, seeks for its separate life away from God, a life that is no life. But the moment the new life is given, the helplessness, the hopelessness, of the struggle is past. The cry of human nature, "I cannot do the things that I would," becomes the thankful utterance of the regenerate soul, "I can do all things through Christ which strengtheneth me;" "For when I am weak, then am I strong;" "And yet not I, but Christ in me."

That thought of sin as a deadly sickness, is surely no mere metaphor. For what is disease in the body but the failure of the organism to perform its functions aright? Life, in the language of biologists, is perfect correspondence to environment, and disease, which is imperfect correspondence, is incipient death. And if, as our heart tells us, God has made us for Himself, made us to find our own true life in Him, then sin is, in a very real sense, like a disease, and leads on to dissolution. In these days, when biological terms are common property, the close parallelism of sin and disease appeals to us, as it did to the Greeks. The Bible has trained us in the thought. The loathsomeness of the leper, the helplessness of the poor paralytic, the wild, self-destroying mania of the possessed, the darkness of the blind, the death in life of those whose limbs are withered,—these are the vivid pictures which the Bible gives us of the sinful soul. Is the parallelism less plain, less terrible, when we turn to the diseases which we know so well? Which of us has not watched by the bedside of the fever-stricken, and marked the rapid pulse, the throbbing brain, the unnatural temperature, the wild, unmeaning eye that looks all strangely on the face it loves, the vague delirious words, with just enough of reason in them to make them terrifying? Such, surely, in the sight of God, is the state of him who, in the full swing of youth and manhood, is living the life of sin. Or, again, who does not know all the terrible stages of consumption, that hopeless malady, which science is powerless to cure or to arrest? Such, in God's sight, ay, and even in man's, is the state of him round whom the bonds of evil habit are slowly closing, like the coils of some giant python, crushing him to death.

And can we find no close analogies in those secret diseases which, long unknown and half-suspected, are feeding their cancerous growth upon our very life? Is anything more painful than to watch the struggle of human strength with the king of terrors? Ah! where there is pain and struggle and effort, there is life, and while there is life there is hope. But a moment comes when there is no struggle. It is all over. And this is *death*. Till then, there were the infinite possibilities of renewed life. At least, we hoped against hope. But now there is no room for hope. We are in the presence of *death.* One little moment has made the momentous change from life to death. And we close the eyelids, and we turn away, and the loved name in our prayers is added to the growing list of those who wait for the mercy of God. Dear brothers and sisters, I dare not do more than suggest the parallel. While the sinful soul struggles, however feebly, with the disease of sin, while it knows pain and suffering and remorse, while it can cast one upward look of unuttered, unutterable prayer to God, there is *life* and there is *hope.* There is no pain when mortification has set in. There is no pain in death. The soul that knows no pain in sinning, that is on easy terms with itself, and has no yearning for God, and purity and holiness, is at least in a deadly swoon. Pray we that God in His mercy will arouse that soul, ay, at the cost of any pain, lest the disease run its course, and sin be perfected in death.

As the work of the Great Reconciler is to prevent the absolute separation of the soul from God, so the work of the Great Physician is to arrest the progress of the disease of sin. To implant in man the supernatural principle of growth and strength, "that thing which by nature man cannot have;" to take up the diseased life into His own perfect life; to destroy death *in* man, as upon the Cross He destroyed it *for* man; this is the regenerating work of Christ, in Whom we are "born again, not of corruptible seed, but of incorruptible, by the Word of God, which liveth and abideth for ever."[1]

[1] 1 Pet. i. 23.

III.

SIN AS THE TRANSGRESSION OF LAW.

"The soul that sinneth, it shall die."—EZEK. xviii. 4.

THERE is a yet deeper thought about sin. It is not only an offence against God, a disease or wound of human nature; it is also *a transgression of an eternal law of right.* Something of this is already, no doubt, implied in the conception of sin as a *debt*, which the debtor cannot pay. But there the legal view predominates, while in the thought of sin as the transgression of law the moral view is uppermost. And while the conception of a creditor who will have payment to the last farthing is utterly alien from the belief in a God of love, the very idea of God requires a vindication of the law of right. It is this which makes men feel that mere forgiveness of sins, the mere treating sin as if it were not, is an impossible thing. God cannot relax the moral law. He did not create it; it is eternal as Himself. Right is not right because God makes it so, but because the moral law is the revelation of God's eternal nature. To rest moral on positive law, Divine or human, is to destroy morality alike in God and man.

And it is the consciousness of an eternal moral law which man has transgressed which lies at the root of the idea of *propitiation.* Man is conscious in himself that he has violated the law of justice; he knows that the violation of that law is death. No forensic fiction, borrowed from human law-courts, no interchange of properties between the sinless and the sinful, can satisfy the conscience. That theory which unbelievers ridicule, conscience and revelation alike reject. When I say, in humble faith, with my eye fixed upon the Cross of Jesus, "I believe in the remission of sins," I mean by forgiveness more, infinitely more, than the passing over of my sin. I believe that my sin is *done away;* that, thanks be to God, I *am righteous* in the sight of God; that He, the All-Holy and the All-Pure, is looking down upon me in love. "Beloved, *now* are we the sons of God." Away with the charitable hypothesis and the legal fiction! Christ does not mock the soul in its agony. He delivers me from the penalty by destroying the sin, and making me righteous in the sight of God. He has taken away my ungodliness, and shall find none (Ps. x. 17). The eternal law of righteousness prevails; the eternal law that sin and God are for ever opposed. It is still true as always—how could it be otherwise, while God is God?—that the righteous Lord loveth righteousness, and His countenance will behold the thing that is just. But though the Lord alloweth the righteous, the ungodly, and him that delighteth in wickedness, doth His soul abhor (Ps. xi. 6, 8). The wrath of God, His eternal hatred of sin, such phrases express truly the utter separation between God and evil. *Reconciliation with God is separation from evil.* To be reclaimed from evil is to be made free to approach God. This is Christ's work. In relation to evil, and the bondage to death, it is called *Redemption* or *Deliverance;* in relation to God, it is *Reconciliation.*

"But how should man be just with God?" This is the question, the tormenting question, of the conscience, and it has everywhere been answered by a belief in sacrifice and propitiation. Crude and anthropomorphic in their ideas of God, men who knew Him only as the antithesis of all that was evil in themselves, yet degraded Him to their own level, sought to pacify Him, to persuade Him, by a compensation, to be propitious to them. We call such views immoral, unworthy of God, even grotesque and childish; yet a great moral truth underlay them—the truth that we, as sinners, are alienated from God, are not worthy to approach, unless we can cover our own hatefulness by something with which He is well pleased. It is the fashion in this day to explain away faith as the outcome of superstition. Christianity explains superstition in the light of faith. It was the dim instinctive feeling after God, the longing of the soul, at any cost, to return to Him. Only slowly, even under the teaching of revelation, did men learn what God is, and that even the sacrifices commanded by God Himself were but "shadows of the true," the One Offering, the Eternal Priest, the Divine Victim. And He, the Loving Father, Who, under the Old Testament, educated the Jews in the true meaning of sacrifice, Himself, in His tender mercy, ordained "a full, perfect, and sufficient sacrifice, oblation, and satisfaction," upon the Altar of the Cross, "for the sins of the whole world." Is, then, Christ's death a compensation paid to the Father? Impossible. Away with such an unholy thought! It is treason against the love of God to speak as if the wrath of the Father could rest for one moment upon the well-beloved Son; or as if that mysterious death were needed to win back for sinners the Father's love. Against all such immoral suggestions, it is enough to remind ourselves that the love of God was the *moving cause*, and not the *result* or the *effect* of the death of Christ.

Can we, then, get any nearer to that wonderful word "propitiation"? Can we, in any intelligible sense, speak of Christ's death as an "expiation"? It is here that the mystery of the Atonement culminates; here that the difference between Remission and Regeneration disappears. If we cannot explain it, at least let us be on our guard against theories which explain it away.

I. Speaking, then, on this great mystery, may we not say that the death of Christ, "the Eternal Son of God," teaches us, as nothing else can, what sin is, and how awful is the purity and holiness of God? We begin to see why "remission of sins" belongs so especially to the Death of Christ, rather than to His Incarnation. We begin to see why the Cross is so dear to the pardoned sinner.

> "Is it not strange, the darkest hour
> That ever dawn'd on sinful earth,
> Should touch the heart with softer power
> For comfort, than an angel's mirth?
> That to the Cross the mourner's eye should turn,
> Sooner than where the stars of Christmas burn?"

No, it is not strange, for in the Cross of Calvary I see that finished work, whereby the sins of the past are done away, the wound of nature is healed, freedom from bondage is won, since man is once more reconciled, made just in the sight of God, "accepted in the Beloved."

II. And, then, may we not say again, that by the Sacrifice of the Cross is revealed the infinite Love of God, in vindicating the eternal law, and yet saving man from death? No legal fiction, no mere vicarious sacrifice, can satisfy our conscience, and make us just before God. It was man that sinned, it is man must suffer.

> "Oh! generous love, that He Who smote
> In man for man the foe;
> The double agony in man,
> For man should undergo."

It is a beautiful suggestion of the greatest of the Schoolmen, that the perfect love and obedience of the perfect manhood, taken into God, was to the Father something He loved more than He hated sin. But, in our day, we love rather to think of the summing up of humanity in Christ, the offering up of all the members in Him Who is the Head. So viewed, Christ's death becomes what it has been finely called, "the Amen of humanity" to the righteous law which sin transgressed. "The soul that sinneth, it shall die;" and Christ, the Perfect Man, and man in Him, admits the justice of that law. So is the eternal law vindicated; so is the Father once more well pleased as He looks on man in His well-beloved Son; so to men and angels God shows Himself "just, and the Justifier of him that believeth in Jesus."

But there is nothing of *substitution*, or imputed righteousness, in all this. Christ died as our Sponsor, our Representative, the Head of the human race, the Second Adam, the Firstborn of redeemed humanity, that we in heart and will might be one with Him in Death and Resurrection. It is as false in theology as it is dangerous to morality to say to the sinner, "You have nothing to do, for Christ has done all for you." Rather would it be true to say, "Christ has died for you that you may die in Him. Christ has done all for you that you may live in Him. He has won for you 'the grace of repentance' (S. Clement). He has offered the one perfect sacrifice of humanity that you and I may be able, in union with It, to offer ourselves to God, and to *know* that 'with such sacrifices God is well pleased.'"

But if the Sacrifice of Christ be external to us, it will avail us nothing. If it is only a fact in the world's history, but not a fact in the history of our own lives, His Death and Resurrection will *for us* have been in vain. We must be crucified with Him, buried with Him in Baptism, that we may rise in Him to newness of life. Suffering in His sufferings, that we may also be glorified together. He did not suffer for us, that we, with a few meaningless words about "faith only," might live a life of ease, perhaps of sin; but that we, being reconciled to God by the Blood of Christ, might live the life of faith, the life of union with the Son of God.

The whole of S. Paul's theology is gathered up and centred in those words, "*in Christ Jesus.*" "There is therefore now no condemnation to them which are *in Christ Jesus.*" And who are they?

They who, having been grafted into the body of the Risen Lord, have been offered up to God in the Sacrifice of Christ; they who, quickened to a new and supernatural life, receiving the Remission of sins by spiritual regeneration, who, in what some call "conversion," have realized in their own souls the greatness of the Baptismal Gift, and have surrendered themselves to that new Life which now throbs in every vein, and kills down the disease of sin; they who, in the Sacrament of Love, are ever offering up themselves anew, body, soul, and spirit, in union with the perfect Sacrifice of Calvary, and drawing thence new strength and life.

Oneness with the Perfect Man—to be bone of His bone and flesh of His flesh—that is the great truth of the sacramental life. To be a living member in His body, the new life nourished and sustained by the mysterious complex of joints and bands, which unite the members with the Head; to be built, as living stones, into that ever-growing building of which Christ is the Foundation and the Corner-stone; to recover ever more and more, under the touch of the Divine Artist's Hand, the lost lineaments of that true Humanity which was made in the image of God; in the strength and power of regenerate manhood, to walk before God in newness of life;—this is to be "in Christ Jesus." This is to participate in the Sacrifice of the Cross and the Resurrection-life. This is to be a link in that unbroken chain—"All things are yours; for ye are Christ's, and Christ is God's."

IV.

SIN AS A DEBT.

"There was a certain creditor which had two debtors: the one owed five hundred pence, and the other fifty. And when they had nothing to pay, he frankly forgave them both."—S. LUKE vii. 41, 42.

IT is not enough to think of sin as "the wound of nature" which needs a Healer. Our conscience testifies to the fact that it is not only a restoration in our present nature that we need, it is a cancelling of the past. If it had only been the regeneration of humanity which was necessary for our reconciliation with God, then, surely, when, in the Incarnation, that nature was taken into God, the work was finished. But we have misread our Bible, nay, we have misread the teaching of our own conscience, if we are satisfied with this. We have misread our Bible, if we do not realize the fact that a mysterious efficacy attaches to the *Death* of Christ. And we read our conscience wrongly if we imagine that we may ignore the past, and, even with the supernatural grace of God, begin as if sin had never been. False theories of human devising have driven us, in this day, to see the Atonement in the light of the Incarnation, rather than the Incarnation as a means to the Atonement. But we may not put the Manger in the place of the Cross, or worship at Bethlehem, and forget Gethsemane and Calvary. It is often said that "*the Remission of sins, if it stood alone, would leave man unsaved.*"[1] Yes; but Regeneration without the Remission of sin, if it were possible, would leave man still unreconciled. But you cannot part them except in thought. The receiving of the Divine pardon is inseparable from the restoration of human nature. Hence, for those who come to be baptized, whether as children or as adults, we pray that they "may receive remission of their sins by spiritual regeneration."[2] The gift of Baptism is twofold, as is the work of Christ. He Who delivers our feet from falling, is He Who delivers our soul from death.

It is this thought of the necessity of *forgiveness* as well as of *regeneration*, which is emphasized by those who have spoken of sin as primarily *a debt or a state of indebtedness to God.* Yet, in the Bible, sin is rarely spoken of in this way. If we except the phrase, "Forgive us our debts, as we forgive our debtors," the only important passages we can quote are the two parables in which God is likened to a lord whose servants owed him a debt they could not pay. In both cases, the fact emphasized is the *remission* of the debt. In the one case, the master "frankly forgave" his servants; in the other, at the servant's prayer, he was moved with compassion, and loosed him, and

[1] Dale, "The Atonement," p. 336.

[2] "Lavacro regenerationis remittuntur cuncta peccata" (S. Aug., "Contra Julianum," II. viii. § 23; ap. Norris, "Rudiments of Theology," p. 297).

forgave him the debt.[1] It would have seemed as if such passages could only have been appealed to in proof of the freedom of God's love in pardoning the sinner, or of the need of the sinner (because he has nothing to pay) of God's mercy and compassion. But it is a far other use which has been made of this metaphor of sin as debt. The jurists of the Middle Ages seized upon the metaphor and interpreted it in the terms of Roman law. How, they asked, is Remission of sins possible? What is the debt man owes? to whom? by whom is it paid? The answer is, man owes to God honour and worship; sin is a robbery of God. But since all that man has and is, is owed to God, he can never repay the debt. And the penalty is death. But Christ has freed man from this debt. He has paid the price of sin, and won forgiveness for us by His death. "Sin is nothing," says S. Anselm, "but the not rendering to God what is due" ("Cur Deus," i. xi.). But that debt to God, which man refused, must be paid, and satisfaction must also be rendered to God for the insult offered to Him. God cannot in justice remit the penalty of sin, else He would put the sinner and the sinless on a level, and admit the sinner to the Presence of Him Whose eyes cannot behold iniquity. Hence Christ, by dying, paid for us debtors a debt which He owed not.[2]

There are great and vital truths hidden in the Schoolman's teaching about sin: (*a*) the truth that

[1] "Necessaria est igitur homini peccatorum remissio ut ad beatitudinem perveniat" ("Cur Deus Homo," i. x.).

[2] S. Aug., "De Trin.," xiii. c. 14; ap. Norris, "Rudiments of Theology," p. 301.

man cannot, by anything that he can do, win the remission of sin, and yet that without that remission, even a holy life, if it were possible, would be of no avail. And then (β) again, it expressed the great truth that the conscience cannot conceive of a mere passing over of sins. There must be something more than the mere refusing to punish. There must be a destruction of the sin. The sinful soul, with all the burden of sin upon it, as it lifts itself up to the Crucified, must see there the handwriting which is against it nailed, as it were, to the Cross. The debt cancelled, because it is paid, not *by* men, but *for* man, in the Sacrifice of Christ.

But the dead hand of legalism rests upon that attempted explanation. It is the least helpful, and, at the same time, the most easily abused of all the many theories of the Atonement. Though S. Anselm never loses sight of the unity of will in the Father and the Son, in the work of man's salvation, the question is not, How is man reconciled to God? but, How is God reconciled to man? And already the suggestion of a transaction, if not a bargain, between the Father and the Son has appeared, and the inexorableness of the Divine Justice is appealed to, to show the necessity of Christ's work. It was reserved for the irreverent hand of sixteenth-century heresy to take up that theory, and to turn it into one, which shocks alike our sense of justice and our belief in the love of God,—to separate the Persons of the ever-blessed Trinity, and play off the love of the Son against the justice of the Father, and by a clumsy theory of imputation to credit the Sinless One with sin, that the sin-stained soul may claim the holiness of God. In that hard and cruel theory of the Atonement, which is associated with the names of Luther and Calvin—the main theological cause, be it remembered, of the unbelief of our day—the lord of the parable who frankly forgave the debt, is transformed into the exacting creditor, who must have all that is "written in the bond," whose last word is, "Pay me that thou owest, even to the uttermost farthing;" but who cares not, if the debt is paid, whether the innocent or the guilty suffer. The unitarianism of Servetus and Socinus, and many a modern "theist," is the protest of the conscience against such an immoral view of God—a protest never more boldly stated than in the well-known words of John Stuart Mill, "I will call no being good, who is not what I mean when I apply that epithet to my fellow-creatures." [1]

Yet, if we can divest it of its legal setting, the thought of sin as debt to God which man can never pay, and which involves the penalty of death, covers a truth which we cannot afford to lose. As against all theories of human merit, I believe in the Remission of sins. I believe in Him Who has taken away the sins of the world. I believe in the finished work of Calvary, as I believe in the progressive work of regeneration. "Being reconciled to God through the death of His Son," we believe that we shall be "saved by His life." "For He Who spared not His own Son, but delivered Him up for us all, how shall

[1] Mill on Hamilton, p. 103.

He not with Him also freely give us all things?" How the remission of sins is possible, is a mystery I cannot fathom. Certainly it is not explained by a theory which makes it immoral and incredible. But I cannot silence the cry for forgiveness which goes up from the heart to a loving God, or work out the belief in a pardon won for me by the precious Blood. I cannot fathom the counsel of the All-Holy. But this I know, God is LOVE, and the Judge of all the earth must do right. It is not for me to justify the ways of God. Enough that "He is faithful and just to forgive us our sins, and to cleanse us from all unrighteousness." "Just, and the Justifier of him that believeth in Jesus." "Forgiving all our iniquities," as well as "healing all our diseases." Irreverent curiosity is the fruitful mother of heresies. Enough that Remission of sins is mine of *mercy*, not of *right*, and that it comes to me from the infinite love of God through the Sacrifice of Calvary.

When I go to the altar of God, the God of my joy and gladness, I will dare to put away from me those curious questionings as to the mode and manner of the Eucharistic Presence. It is enough for me to know that Christ is there. "O my God, Thou art there; O my soul, thou art happy."

And as I kneel on Good Friday before the Cross of Jesus, I will dare to do the same. What was the stern demand of Divine justice, I know not, or whether some other act of love might not have won for man forgiveness. One thing I know. Whereas I was once weighed down by the burden of sin, it has fallen from me as I knelt before the Cross, and I believe in the Remission of sins.

Once more, in the solemn hour of dying, I will dare to put aside theories and cling to fact. I turn from Anselm the Schoolman to Anselm the saint. Listen to what he says: "If the Lord thy God wills to judge thee, say, 'O Lord, between me and Thy judgment I present the Death of our Lord Jesus Christ; no otherwise can I contend with Thee.' And if He shall say that thou art a sinner, say thou, 'O Lord, I interpose the Death of our Lord Jesus Christ between my sins and Thee.' If He says that He is wroth with thee, say, 'Lord, I oppose the Death of Jesus Christ between Thy wrath and me.' And when thou hast completed, say again, 'Lord, I set the Death of Jesus Christ, my Saviour, between Thee and me.'"

"Look, Father, look on His anointed Face,
And only look on us as found in Him;
Look not on our misusings of Thy grace,
Our prayer so languid, and our faith so dim;
For lo! between my sins and their reward
I set the Passion of Thy Son, our Lord."

V.

BONDAGE OF SIN.

"Whosoever committeth sin is the slave of sin."—S. JOHN viii. 34.

THERE are many metaphors under which the fact of sin is described to us in the Bible. In its own most real nature, it is the turning away of the soul from God, Who is the Life of our life. But that separation is not at once complete and final. Man feels and knows that he is estranged from God, and longs for union with Him. He knows that he belongs to God, and cannot, will not, believe that God will cast him off for ever. That is why, apart altogether from what we call revelation, and the assured promises of God, man strives to return, to restore himself, to return to his true rest in God. But slowly and truly he realizes the fact that the restoration must come from outside himself, that he needs a Saviour.

It is when he has realized this, that he exhausts every metaphor to bring home to himself his state. Sin is a disease, a deadly disease which, by slow and sure degrees, leads on to inevitable death, unless a Great Physician can point out and remove the hidden cause; and the sufferer cries out at his pain, "Heal my soul; for I have sinned against Thee."

Or, again, he thinks of himself as a debtor lingering under sentence of the law, unable to pay his debt, and therefore, as in the old law, his very life forfeited; and he knows of no remedy but in forgiveness—the cancelling of the debt by Him to Whom the debt is owed.

Or, once more, he is conscious of sin as a bondage. He knows himself to be a slave, and yet one who was born to be free. He is a slave, and knows that he has enslaved himself, and yet he seeks in vain to break his chains. And the cry goes up to the Redeemer, the Ransomer, to Him Who alone can set at liberty them which are bound, and deliver the prisoner from his chains.

It is this view of sin which we are to think of to-night—sin as a bondage and a slavery.

There are two senses in which man, as sinful, is in *bondage*. By the act of sin, he falls under that law of which I spoke yesterday—"The soul that sinneth, it shall die." He has "the sentence of death" in himself. He is "in danger of" final and utter separation from God. He is under the slavery of fear. "Through fear of death he is all his life subject to bondage" (Heb. ii. 15). His spirit is "the spirit of bondage unto fear" (Rom. viii. 15). In Bible language, he is "under a curse." And from that slavery he knows that he cannot deliver himself, or make that expiation which the moral law demands. It is in relation to that bondage, that the Death of Christ is called a *Redemption*, and a ransom from death. The ancient promise, "I will *ransom* thee from the power of the grave; I will *redeem* thee from destruction,"[1] is fulfilled in Him Who "came to give His Life a ransom for many,"[2] or, as S. Paul dares to say, "A ransom for all, to be testified in due time."[3]

But there is another sense in which man as a sinner is in bondage. He is not only subject to the penalty of sin, he is also, in a very real sense, *the slave of sin.* The separation from God is not merely an act which offends God, it implies a wound of nature which is typified by disease; it not only in itself needs an expiation, it requires a deliverance from the consequences; it involves an *ἀταξία.* "He that committeth sin is the slave of sin" (S. John viii. 34). He is "the slave of corruption: for of whom a man is overcome, of the same is he brought in bondage" (2 Pet. ii. 19). In reference to this bondage, also, Christ's work is a Redemption, a reclaiming of man for God. The curse of sin being removed, man is no longer *de jure* the servant of sin. He is free and able; and if he is to continue a slave, it is because he refuses to assert his freedom, to emancipate himself.

These two different senses in which the words "bondage" and "redemption" are used, were not at first clearly distinguished; and it was sometimes maintained that the Death of Christ was the price paid to the devil, as the personal power of evil. The atoning work of Christ was thus degraded to a bargain or transaction between God and the Prince

[1] Hosea xiii. 14. [2] S. Matt. xx. 28; S. Mark x. 45.
[3] 1 Tim. ii. 6.

of Darkness; as afterwards, in Reformation days, it was degraded to a bargain between the Father and the Son. The noble protest of S. Gregory of Nazianzen against this view is well known, but it is worth repeating. "If," he says, "a ransom goes by right to him who holds that which is to be ransomed, I ask to whom was the ransom paid, and for what reason? If you say it was paid to the Evil One—out upon the injurious thought! What! the robber receive not merely a ransom from God, but God Himself as ransom! Truly a monstrous compensation for his tyranny, to oblige him to spare such creatures as we are!"[1]

But it was not the moral protest of S. Gregory, but the legal reasoning of S. Anselm, which finally discredited this false view, when he showed that, whatever satisfaction meant, it was owed not to the devil, but to the eternal law of righteousness. It is only in this sense, that we can speak of man being redeemed from bondage by a ransom paid by Christ. And, in this sense, the Redemption is a part of the atoning work of Christ.

But it is of the second kind of slavery that I would speak to-day. "He that committeth sin is the slave of sin." And this thought, that we are slaves, touches us very nearly. For the name of freedom is precious in English ears. Ever since the days when Wilberforce saved our country from participation in a cruel and hateful traffic, the noblest feelings of our nature vibrate at the name of liberty

[1] Orat. xlii. ap. Norris, p. 303.

—personal liberty, political liberty, intellectual liberty. Are they not our glory? It is a proud, almost an insolent boast of ours, that "Britons never will be slaves," and that every slave is free whose foot is set on English soil. Would God it were so! Look around you and see. I dare not trust myself to speak of the cruelty and horror of that white-slave trade which is being carried on here in our very midst, or to remind you that to tolerate slavery in others, is to undermine the whole edifice of freedom. But look at the slaves of drunkenness, and the slaves of lust, and the slaves of gold, and the slaves of sloth, and the slaves of frivolity, and the slaves of fashion, and the slaves of self-love. We are almost tempted to quote, in a new meaning, the opening words of the author of the "Social Contract." "Man is born free, and he is everywhere in chains." And the hopelessness of it all is, that we Englishmen, with our big words about freedom, have so inadequate a view of what true freedom is. Why, it has almost passed into a proverb, that an Englishman's freedom is having his own way, and doing as he pleases. Can any view of freedom be more false and hollow. "Who," asks S. Basil, "is free?" The man "who is his own master." There is no such "being amongst men." If he is not the servant of God, he is the slave of sin. We understand that state of bondage in which a man struggles vainly against some degrading sin, yielding again and again to some petty temptation, powerless against unworthy habit. "He is a slave, and he knows it," and the misery of bondage is increased by the misery of self-contempt, and the loss of self-respect. "What I would, that do I not: but what I hate, that do I" (Rom. vii. 15). "O wretched man that I am! who shall deliver me from the body of this death?" (Rom. vii. 24). That bondage we see and pity, or we feel and despise ourselves for it. Sin means much more than this. But what of those chains that men bear so easily? What of the "false freedom" of him whose aimless life is at the mercy of chance desires, who lives on vaguely in the hope that "something will turn up," who suffers his will to be determined by circumstances, his morality by his next-door neighbour, his intellectual position by the newspapers? What of the thousands in this great city who are toiling out their lives in mere money-making? What of those who, knowing that their talents, or their natural genius, fit them for something higher, yet are content to degrade themselves to a life of bondage? Remember that the cruelty and suffering which we commonly associate with slavery is not its essential quality. *That which really constituted slavery is that it is a moral evil;* that it maims and degrades human nature in that in which it is most like God; that it disfranchises man of his rights as a citizen in God's world. And everything which draws us down, or away from our own true human life, is a slavery, even if it be not felt; ay, all the more, if the slavery is mistaken freedom. The last and hopeless stage of separation from God is that of the soul which no longer desires God or feels remorse at sin: the last and hopeless stage in disease is that in which there is no pain, no struggle, no effort, for it is a state of death; and this, the last most hopeless state of bondage, is that of the slave who hugs his chains, and fancies he is free.

What, then, is true freedom? Not the being without a master, or the being one's own master. That is impossible. Not the doing as one likes; for some have come to like slavery. We cannot escape service. But there is a service which is bondage, and a service which is perfect freedom. The lawless life is no more free than the life lived at the beck and call of some external power. That often-abused term, "the freedom of the will," is not a liberty of indifference, but a power of self-emancipation from that which is alien from our best, our truest self. The life of passion, the life of self-indulgence, the life frittered away in mere time-killing, is no more our true life than the life of chains and prison walls. To live that life is to be a slave. And he only is free who is living his own true life; not the wayward and irresolute life of pleasure, or the capricious life of self-will, but the strong free life of duty and obedience to the Will of God, welcomed as our own true good.

Self-emancipation! Are you slaves or free? Have you won self-emancipation? You cannot compel a man to be free. You cannot make him free in spite of himself. Twice were the Israelites in bondage, in Egypt and in Babylon, and God raised up for them deliverers, released them from external restraint, that they might become really free. And, for a little while, they seemed to value that freedom; seemed grateful for that Redemption which they longed for when they who hated them were lords over them. And then they lapsed into slavery again, proved themselves unworthy to be free, by abandoning the service of God for the slavery of an idolatrous or superstitious worship.

Of how many souls the same is true! We are born to be free, born with at least some natural power to struggle against the bondage of sin, born with the knowledge that we are not meant for slaves, and as Christians born again in Holy Baptism, and gifted with the power to be free. But soon we feel how weak we are, how quickly drawn away to evil, how easily our will gives up the struggle, how terrible is the weight of sin, and yet how hopeless it is for our unaided strength to strive against it. Our conscience tells us that a man is the slave of his natural desires, only in so far as he yields to them; but it is so easy to yield, so hard to struggle, and we just let things go.

And what is true of the will in its relation to the temptation of our lower nature, is true of the reason in relation to ignorance. We talk of the slavery of ignorance, and of the freedom of truth. But do we know that here, too, the freedom has to be won? Free thought is not the liberty of adopting some ready-made arguments against revelation. The only thought that is free is that which lays hold on truth, whether in the natural or the spiritual world. To know the truth about Nature is to assert our rightful lordship over her—to establish a true relation between man and the external world; and to know the truth about God, is to claim our right relation to Him Whose service alone is perfect freedom.

Christ came to make us free, and break the bonds of slavery which separate us either by sin or ignorance. What has Christ done for human freedom in the moral and intellectual world? He has not only broken the bonds in which we were held. He has done what no human deliverer can do. He has given the liberated slaves the spirit of freedom, the power to be free. He has given to human nature (in union with His own free and perfect manhood) the power to overcome the slavery of sinful habit. He has given mankind, in the revelation of the Father, a truth that sets man free—free in the freedom of reclaimed humanity, free in the victory over enslaving sin, free in the glad service of a loving Father.

Stand fast, therefore, in the liberty with which Christ has made us free. Ye were the servants of sin once, the servants of ignorance once, the servants of your own mere wayward selves. Be not entangled again with the yoke of bondage, the bondage of evil or vicious habit, of mere undisciplined fancy, of a life not yet recognized as a true vocation, and worthy of your real selves. The regenerating power of Christ's life in you gives you the right to answer every argument for slavery with an indignant protest—"I was free born."

For the Christian there is no slavery but the unwillingness to be free; no ignorance but the despair of truth. And hence there is no life—unless it be a

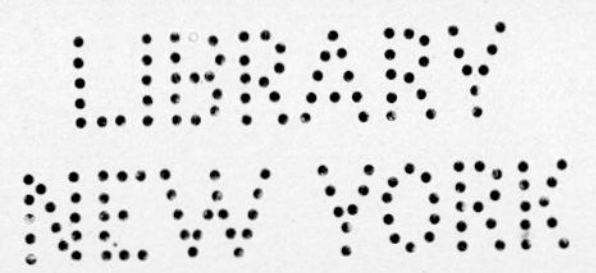

life of sin—no life, however servile it may seem, which may not be the sphere for the development of the true human personality, the will strengthened, the reason enlightened, the whole man enfranchised by the grace of God, able to say, This life that I am living, this little bit of work that I am trying to do as well as I can, is a real work for God and man. It is worthy of a true, free, human activity. All that looks, to the outside world, dreary routine; unprofitable and perishing labour; dull, and uninteresting, and commonplace;—is that by which God is enabling me to win my freedom, my victory over sin, the world, and self. I do not envy the "unchartered freedom" of a purposeless and undirected life. It is to me as the bondage of the life of sin. There is no freedom but the power to live the true life of humanity, the life of free and fearless union with the Father; *the reconciliation perfected, the wound of nature healed, the debt cancelled, the atonement made, the bondage broken.* The Eternal Son has set me free, that I may be free indeed.

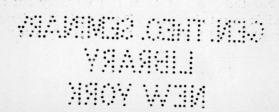

III.

COURSE OF SERMONS

Preached in Lincoln Cathedral, in Holy Week, 1889

on

THE DISCIPLES AND THEIR LORD

I.

THE BETRAYAL.

"What will ye give me, and I will deliver Him unto you?"
S. MATT. xxvi. 15.

WE meet together, as disciples of Jesus Christ, in this Holy Week, in order that we may learn more of the love of God, and realize in that knowledge more of the sin of man; and that, as we kneel before the Cross, with our eyes upon the Crucified, we may see and know what we really are in His sight.

And it seemed to me it might help us to this knowledge, if, in these first three days, we were to set before ourselves, and think specially of, the Twelve Disciples and their relations with the Master. For they were, as we are, an inner circle of Christ's followers. Of the many who listened to His words, some were offended and turned away, some were elevated but not changed, some were drawn to Him and would even have been His Disciples, if they could have served Him without cost. Some were recognized as Disciples, like the seventy, and commissioned by Christ to do His work. But the Twelve were "chosen," "chosen out of the world," kept very near to Christ Himself, instructed in the mysteries of the new kingdom by the King Himself. Slowly, and as they were able to bear it, He unfolded to them the future—the paradox of a Kingdom founded by the death of its King, the paradox of a Society which was "in the world, yet not of the world," the paradox of the Judge of all condemned by a human tribunal, the paradox of the Son of Man "lifted up" upon the Cross by the sons of men, and, greatest paradox of all, the Master Whom they knew and loved, betrayed, forsaken, denied by His chosen friends.

And as we are inclined, at first, to suppose that those who were chosen to be Christ's Disciples must have been different from common men, so, when we hear of their fall, we are ready to say, How cruel! how impossible! If we had been admitted to that sacred fellowship, heard those gentle, loving words, and drunk in all the strange mystery of that wonderful life, we should have been—indeed, who could fail to be?—unworthy of it. But at least we could not have done as they did—betrayed, deserted, denied the Master in the hour of His loneliness. Oh, brothers, human nature is now what it was then. The fellowship with Christ, and the call to be His disciples, is still the touchstone of character. The same Lord has called us in Holy Baptism. "Ye have not chosen Me, but I have chosen you," He seems to say once more. And He is revealing to us now the mystery of His Kingdom, as, to the Twelve, He revealed the mystery of His earthly life. And that revelation is a disenchantment, a disillusionment, a disappointment to all that is earthly and selfish in our hopes. Who is the Christ we believe in, and love? The Christ of Jewish expectation, or the Christ of Calvary? The Christ whom the world to-day professes itself ready to worship? or the Christ whom the world hates, and will hate to the end? "What think ye of Christ?" is still the test-question of each life.

We can hardly be wrong in supposing that "the Twelve" shared in the Jewish expectation that the Messiah would be a temporal King, Who should trample on the pride of imperial Rome, and set up a visible Messianic rule. And we can trace the stages by which the higher Christian idea was unfolded to them. It came, that revelation, in a series of disappointments. First, the death of the Baptist, the great prophet of the Messiah; then the refusal by Christ to commit Himself to the enthusiasm of those who would have made Him a King. What did it mean? Is He not a King? Will He never assert Himself? Can a kingdom be won by these constant withdrawals, these refusals, as it were, to fight? Every new opportunity seemed to bring its new discouragement. Christ avoids or evades the challenge to manifest Himself to the world. Then came the crisis, as it were, the open challenge to prove His Messiahship by a "sign." Surely He must accept it—He Who had appealed to the evidence of His own wonderful work, when questioned by the Disciples of John. Surely now, if ever, is the moment to legitimate His claim, and manifest Himself unto the world. And once more the challenge is refused. To the Pharisees He seemed to have failed, even to have admitted His defeat. No sign shall be given. To the Disciples it was one more bitter lesson of disappointment.

Yet that gospel of progressive disillusionment, the gradual stripping off of all that was false and earthly in Jewish Messianic ideas, was a revelation of the True Messiah, the Eternal Word, God manifest in the flesh. And that revelation was a testing of the character of the chosen Twelve, just as there is a testing of the character of Christians to-day, when once more we are being told that Christianity is a failure, and that the religion of the Cross is outgrown.

In trying to fix our thoughts on the different ways in which the Disciples were affected by Christ's revelation of Himself, there is a real danger that we should forget how much they were like ourselves; how, in fact, they show to us, as it were, types of character, clearly discernible to-day, amongst ourselves. It is easy to represent to ourselves Judas the traitor, as a moral monster, and the Disciples as cowardly, half-hearted followers of Christ, and S. Peter as one whose self-confidence prepared the way for his fall. But, to do this, is to lose the lesson of their lives, and to fail to read there the steps by which character is formed by the Revelation of God.

Let us take first the character of the traitor Judas. Three times, in the Gospel narrative, is Judas said to have been, in some special sense, the devil's instrument. And the first occasion was a year before the actual betrayal. "Have not I chosen you twelve, and one of you is a devil?" What did it mean? Already, to the eye of Christ, there was seen the line of moral cleavage between the one and the eleven. Together they had received the uniform teaching of "discouragement," together they had realized what must have seemed to all alike, the failure of Christ, the break-down of His Messianic claim, at least, in the form in which they had been accustomed to think of it. Together they had been compelled to make their choice. Of those who had followed Christ, "many were offended," and the pathetic appeal to the chosen Twelve is heard, "Will ye also go away?" No. They will throw in their lot, even if it must be with a lost cause. Even in despondency, and almost despair, they are ready to fling away the cherished hope of ambition, of personal gain, and cling to Him they loved. And yet not all. One has in secret made a different choice. He is still in external union with them. But he had fought for his own hand, when he joined what he thought the winning side, and he will fight for his own hand now that he foresees its failure—not openly, but secretly; in outward friendship and companionship, but with secret alienation of heart. He was amongst the Disciples, but, though perhaps they did not know it, he is no longer one of them. "Have not I chosen you twelve, and one of you is a devil?"

So the old sin of Paradise is repeated. The act

which at heart all sin is, the self-love which separates man from God and makes him try to live and stand alone. "It is the essence of immorality," says a great moral teacher of our own day, "to make one's self an exception." Judas made himself an exception, fought for his own hand; determined, if the cause was lost, that he at least would not be altogether a loser. Disappointed ambition dropped so naturally into its lower, baser form of covetousness. Then began that life of unreality, and hypocrisy, and deceit. The petty thefts from the common store which, as steward of the Apostolic College, he was entrusted with, were but an indication of the perfect separation which he had made between his own interests and that of his Master and his brethren. Already, in heart and will, he was a traitor. For treachery has no meaning but the working against some cause or person to which openly we profess a loyal allegiance.

How well we know the later stages in that miserable life! and what we do not know, imagination finds it easy to supply. Twice, we are told, "Satan entered into Judas," and, in each case, the occasion was of some gracious act of love and condescension for the Lord he professed to serve. (*a*) Once when, as Mary's loving hand poured precious ointment on the sacred feet, and He to Whom she ministered, accepted and interpreted her gift ("she did it for My burial"), and checked the words of him whose petty covetousness found fault with the "waste." Then, first, the treachery, which was hidden in the heart of

Judas, took shape, and he bargained for his price: "What will ye give me?" Surely there was more of malice, and disappointment, and hatred, than of covetousness, in the words; else he would have asked for more than the slave's ransom, just thirty half-crowns of our money, as though in insolent contempt of her who thought three times that sum too little for the offering of love, the anointing of Jesus' feet. (β) Then, at the Last Supper, once more Satan entered into the traitor, and claimed him as his own. The Master had washed the traitor's feet. Judas had heard his treachery foretold, "One of you shall betray Me," as if in that last hour the appeal of love must be made; and he answered with the hypocritical "Is it I?" Then came those awful words, which left the sinner to his sin, "That thou doest, do quickly." And he went out into the darkness. Then, in quick succession, we recall the garden meeting, the traitorous kiss, the remorseful "I have sinned, for I have betrayed!" and the scornful "See thou to that!" And Judas the traitor *stood alone.* He had thought, at least, to take care of himself, to look out for his own interests, to this end, whatever might happen. He had sacrificed all to that—Master, friends, the respect of his own conscience, and of men. He has fought for his own hand. He has got his way. He is alone now, awfully alone; *alone* in the presence of God and of his sin; *alone*, for his treachery had separated him from his Master and his brethren; *alone*, for the high priests hate and despise their miserable tool; *alone*, for the crowds who will soon shout, "Crucify, crucify!"

have no word of sympathy for the false friend, the hypocrite, the thief, the betrayer. And in his ears those words keep ringing, "What shall it profit a man if he gain the whole world?" What shall it profit? And forth he rushes into the darkness, to hide himself from himself, away across the Valley of Hinnom, to the Field of Blood. And that weird solitude witnessed the last act of him whom after-times look back upon as the hypocrite, the thief, the traitor, the suicide!

It all seems so ghastly and so horrible, so far removed from our life that we live now, we who profess and call ourselves Christians, who wear upon our foreheads the Cross of Baptism, and have come to decorate our churches with, or to wear as an ornament, that which, to men of Christ's time, was what the gallows is in ours—a necessary, but dismal piece of social machinery. We have idealized the Cross. Are we in any real sense the Disciples of the Crucified? We are so ready to take things for granted, so ready to forget, what we know so well, the intimate blending of deceit and self-deceit, by which the hypocrisy, assumed to deceive others, soon comes to deceive no one but the hypocrite.

And it almost seems as if, in our day, Christ was leading His Church through the same description of disappointment through which He led His Disciples. We are told from outside that Christianity has failed. And, if we accept and apply the world's test of what failure is, we must admit that it is true. Christianity has not introduced a golden age. It has not absorbed the world into itself. If it is moving on to its goal, that goal must be something different from what the world means by success. But we are thinking, not of the outside world, but of ourselves. Are there Judases among the chosen ones? Have we, any of us, who are signed with the Cross, and have received the Seal of the Lord, nay, who have been brought into closest, truest union with Him in the Sacrament of His Love, been sometimes disquieted, sometimes despondent, at the failure of Christianity? If so, what then? For it is here that we come to the dividing of the ways, the line which separates the followers of the Crucified from those who would be Christians without the Cross.

It is so secret, so subtle, that treachery. We do not mean to oppose the Christianity we profess. We mean, in a general way, to be loyal to it. But it wants resetting. That is the modern phase. It must be widened so as to include new ideas. It cannot go on in antagonism to what seems to be the onward movement of civilization. And, little by little, we advance. We pare down this truth, and explain away that. And then we get impatient with those people—very good, no doubt, but so old-fashioned, so uncompromising, so almost defiant in their faith. Do not misunderstand me. I am not thinking of new truths, whether of science, or criticism, or political and social life. The religion of Jesus Christ has room enough for these. I am thinking of new and laxer views of what a religious life means, of what morality requires, of the respect to be paid to the opinion of the world.

These are the things towards which the religion of Christ is defiant and uncompromising. And we begin by little thefts from God and man. Surely we need not be quite so strict, quite so hard with ourselves, quite so firm in the face of evil! We want to see good in everything, even in evil. And we play with sin and familiarize ourselves with it. And the stern, unbending holiness and purity of the Gospel begins to seem unreal; too high, at least, for the world as we know it. And we resent the attempt to enforce that higher view. We have a programme of our own. We are going to broaden the laws of Christianity. We are going to make it more comprehensive. And we begin to talk about rehabilitation, and a new reformation. We want to get rid of everything which any one can object to, and to modernize Christianity, which means abandoning that whereby its victory hitherto has been secured. And before we know it, we are parleying with Christ's enemies. "What will ye give me, and I will deliver Him unto you?" Slowly we have separated our interests from His. We thought to unite Christ and the world, to make the most of both. We did not believe that they were diametrically opposed, and we realize it only when we have become hopelessly identified with the cause that is not His.

It is only one step further in self-deceit when we try and defend, to ourselves or to others, the treachery we have been guilty of, or look round to see what private gain or fame or money we make out of the betrayal of the faith. An article in a review, a society novel, a graphic picture of a soul's tragedy,—these are the short cuts to notoriety nowadays. It is the way in which we at once conceal our treachery, and satisfy ambition, and throw a kind of intellectual halo over moral cowardice or sloth.

Brethren, Christ has many open enemies; but it is amongst the baptized that the traitors are found, and the darkest treachery is that of those who have been brought very near their Lord. Therefore "let him that thinketh he standeth take heed lest he fall." "Nowhere," says S. Bernard, "are pilgrims in perfect safety. Not in Heaven, for Lucifer fell from thence; not in Paradise, for Adam was driven thence; much less in the world, since Judas perished in the school of Christ." Let us therefore *fear*. The beginning of treachery is that which we know so well, and fear so little—unreality in religion; and the beginning of unreality is the separation of faith from life, or faith from thought. A faith which no longer shows itself in a holy life, a faith which we keep hidden away apart from all that appeals to our rational nature, is a faith to which we are already false—which, when the occasion offers, we shall be ready to betray. A divided allegiance is itself a treachery, for we cannot serve two masters.

Be very watchful, then, against self-deceit, very suspicious of religious shams, unreal professions, and unmeaning truths. The beginnings of disloyalty are so secret, and the progress of self-deceit so gradual, and the allurements of the world, the flesh, and the devil, so cunningly disguised, that, even while we think ourselves the servants of Christ, we may be already traitors to our Lord.

As we read again the story of the Disciple who became a traitor, we dare not, any of us, put aside as impossible the thoughts of treachery,—"Is it I?"

II.

THE DESERTION.

"Then all the disciples forsook Him, and fled."—S. MATT. xxvi. 56.

WE traced yesterday the steps by which Judas, the chosen Disciple, became the betrayer of his Lord. We saw how slowly, as the mystery of Christ's earthly life was revealed to His Disciples, and they learned that it was no earthly kingdom and no worldly triumph that was in store for His followers, but defeat, and shame, and suffering, and death,—Judas has in heart and will, and finally by overt act, separated himself from the Disciples of Christ. That self-love, which lies at the heart of all sin, had had in him its full development. First it showed itself in ambition; then in the meaner vice of covetousness; then in hypocrisy and unreality, deceit and treachery; and then the awful climax of self-hatred and despair, the death of the suicide.

To-day we turn to the other Disciples, to see how their character was formed under the same discipline of disappointment.

For they too started, as Judas did, with high hopes of an earthly kingdom. Had not the Master even seemed to encourage it, when He had promised that "in the regeneration" they should sit on thrones judging the twelve tribes of Israel? What could this "regeneration" mean but a renovated theocratic Judaism, which should lord it over the Roman tyrant, and draw Gentiles to its light, and kings to the brightness of its rising?

Then there came, as if to dash their hopes, those many withdrawings of the Lord—His repeated refusals to assert Himself, or allow others to declare His greatness; His final failure, as it seemed, to meet the challenge of the Pharisees. It was then that the traitorous heart of Judas began to separate him from the rest, to seek his own aggrandizement. He too had felt the disappointment, the failure, the sickness of hope deferred, and he was already making his plans.

Yet it was out of the very heart of disappointment and failure, when many of the outer circle of Disciples went back, and "walked no more with Him," that there came that wonderful confession of faith, "Thou art the Christ of God." It was, St. John tells us, the answer to that appeal, "Will ye also go away?" that S. Peter, as the mouthpiece of the Disciples, replied, "Lord, to whom shall we go? Thou hast the words of eternal life." It was a victory won through despondency, almost despair—a victory which grew more sure, as it became more conscious of the moral basis on which it rested. "Thou hast the words of eternal life. And we believe and are sure"—let the world say what it will, let faltering disciples fail, and traitors prove false and enemies triumph—"we believe and are sure that Thou art that Christ, the Son of the Living God." It was the utterance of a truth which had been learned, not from flesh and blood, but from the Father Himself. In that moment of lofty moral insight, S. Peter rose above himself. The weakness of flesh and blood might afterwards, for a little while, throw into the shade that victory of faith. But it was a victory won on the very field where Judas failed. In his enthusiasm, S. Peter seemed to speak for all; yet some of the Twelve were wavering, and one was already estranged in heart and will: "There are some of you who believe not," and "One of you is a devil." Yet they, who had eyes to see and ears to hear, were permitted, even in what seemed the crisis of defeat, to witness the passing glory of the Transfiguration Mount. The hour of failure had been the moment of moral victory, and prepared for that vision of unearthly glory when the God-Man was revealed.

Yet the discipline of disappointment went on. Nay, from the time of S. Peter's great confession the forewarnings of the Master's sufferings and death became more clear and unmistakable. Not only in parable, as before, does the Master speak now. He has given them the key to His dark sayings. They understand now what it all meant—the children of the bridechamber mourning for the Bridegroom; the Heir cast out of His own vineyard; the good Shepherd giving His life for the sheep; the Cross to be borne; the Flesh to be given for the world's life; the

Son of Man to be buried like a second Jonah. They cannot mistake His meaning. For "from that time forth"—from the time of S. Peter's confession—Christ told how He must suffer at Jerusalem, and be killed, and sternly rebukes, as a suggestion of Satan, the earthly and human desire to hold Him back from suffering. Even amidst the brightness of the Transfiguration-glory, when Moses and Elias were permitted to see and converse with Him, Whom the Law and the Prophets alike foreshadowed, we are told "they spake of His decease which He should accomplish at Jerusalem." And when He came down from the Mount, and healed the demoniac, and the people were amazed, recognizing the mighty power of God, once more the Disciples' rising hopes are dashed by the words, "The Son of Man shall be delivered into the hands of men."

Yet very slowly did the Disciples abandon their ideas of worldly gain and earthly greatness. Once, when the mother of James and John had made a request, or a claim, for special honour for her sons, they resented it; for they too hoped for greatness "in the kingdom." And little did they understand the Master's words to the brothers, "Ye shall drink indeed of My cup, and be baptized with My baptism"—that the greatness, the fellowship in suffering, shall be yours. These are the rewards in the kingdom of the Crucified. And still the Disciples disputed who should be greatest, and could not understand the greatness of childlike obedience, the supremacy of perfect self-committal.

And when at last they realized—as they could not but realize—that their dreams of greatness were but dreams, that Christ's kingdom is not of this world, and that they were walking with their Master along the *via crucis*,—a shade of sadness and weariness and despondency settled down upon them. There is no thought of disloyalty, no idea, as with Judas, of a separate life. Self-love in them had been so far destroyed. They were committed to Christ; their affection was strong enough to cling to Him, if need be, they thought, to die with Him. But as S. Peter had been their mouthpiece in the great confession, so does S. Thomas now give expression to their feeling of despondency and despair. "Let us also go, that we may die with Him." Better to die with Christ than to live without Him.

So much their love was strong enough to dare. But with despondency comes sloth, and with hopelessness the weakening of that faith which had carried them so far. Treachery, denial, desertion, —impossible! Though all should be offended, they will not be offended! And yet, as their lives were no longer sustained by the buoyancy of hope, the kindred virtues of faith and love grow weaker, and the sad acquiescence in the inevitable led to a relaxation of moral effort,—so strangely do despondency and sloth act and react on one another. Only six days after the first clear announcement by Christ of His approaching sufferings and death, the announcement which called forth the impetuous protest of S. Peter, "Be it far from Thee, Lord!" we read that, even on the Transfiguration Mount, those who were, as it seemed, ever an inner circle of the chosen Twelve—Peter and James and John—"were heavy with sleep" (S. Luke ix. 32), and when they woke and saw their Lord with Moses and Elias, their drowsy eyes could not distinguish clearly between the servants and the Son. They would have built three tabernacles—one for Moses, one for Elias, one for Christ. And only when the vision passed, and Jesus was seen alone in the transcendant majesty of Sonship, did they realize how low and earthly had been their thought of Him, how sloth had dulled the vision of the soul.

Pass we to the Garden of Gethsemane. The end was very near now—the moment when the Shepherd should be smitten, and the sheep scattered. Nay, their desertion had been clearly foretold. "All ye shall be offended because of Me this night." Surely they will watch with Him at least till the end, which is so near! Surely love will be strong enough to share that agony! Surely that appeal must be heard—"My soul is exceeding sorrowful, even unto death. Tarry ye here, and *watch* with Me"! But their eyes were heavy, and their hearts were sad, and hope had gone, and dull, helpless resignation had settled down upon their souls. And when the Master returned, He found them sleeping. Yet there is no word of censure, only something of sadness—may we not say, of *disappointment?* "What, could ye not watch *with Me one hour?* Watch and pray, that ye enter not into temptation." Again, and a third time, He comes and finds them sleeping still. They have been tried, and failed. They could not watch. "Sleep on now, and take your rest." It sounds almost like the echo of those words to Judas, "What thou doest, do quickly." The moment of trial is past. It is all over. The only one of the Twelve who was wakeful on that night was Judas the betrayer, who watched, but didn't love. The betrayer is near; and the Disciples, who loved, but could not watch, saw their Master taken; and they who, in the strength of enthusiastic hope, once "forsook all, and followed Him," now, all in panic fear, "forsook Him, and fled." It was but for a little while. There was no thought of treachery or disloyalty in their hearts, only the cowardice and faint-heartedness which comes of despondency and sloth. Two at least will recover themselves before the trial is over; one will even take his stand beneath the Cross, with those brave women whose clinging love could triumph where the boasted strength of men had failed. But for the moment, they fled. They had fallen, and the Master was left alone in the moment of betrayal, as He had been alone in the hour of His agony.

Brethren, can we not see here a true picture of ourselves? We would fain believe that among those who are signed and sealed as the followers of Christ, and who eat with Him at His Altar-Table, the traitors—those who are wilfully and consciously disloyal, the friends who lift up their heel against Him—are very, very few. But what of the cowardly, despondent, faint-hearted Christians? Are they few amongst ourselves? What of the slothful ones who cannot "watch," cannot "endure hardness," who have committed themselves to Christianity as if it were a sort of "forlorn hope" for the world, but haven't the heart to fight for it and believe in it as a conquering power?

In our day there are few arguments more common in the mouth of the enemies of this Faith than the reproach that Christianity is a failure. Look, they say, at a map of the religions of the world. Put on one side, if you will, the nature-worship and the ancestor-worship, polytheism and fetishism and animism, and even those religions which claim to be national. Look only at the three religions which claim to be universal. Look at the five hundred millions of Buddhists, and the hundred and fifty-five millions of Mohammedans. Can you believe that Christianity, represented by some twenty-six per cent. of the human race, if we include all forms of Christianity, is really the religion of man as man; and that, if the Incarnation had been true, Christianity would have had such limited success? Is it reasonable, we are asked, to talk of Christianity as the One Religion?

And not only has Christianity failed, we are told, in its project of converting the world; it has failed within its own area, and in its own territory. To say nothing of the divisions of Christendom, look at the morals of Christian countries. See how few follow, even afar off, the pure and loving Life of the Christ. See how the Church has almost confessedly failed to make her children Christ-like. Can you still believe it?

Or, once more, look at it in your own life. Think of the boasted "consolations of Christianity:" hasn't it failed there too? Can you really say that your religion lifts you out of the reach of those ills which flesh is heir to? Isn't it the very few who know the "joy of salvation"?

Ah, how well we know the argument! And hasn't it sometimes, even while we resented it and put it away from us, reacted on our belief, and made us sad and half-hearted and hopeless? And if the personal devotion to Him Who loved us and redeemed us with His own Blood still holds us true to Him in the bonds of affection, yet somehow the heart has gone out of our work, and we are more ready to let things go, and to sit and wait. And that admission of despondency, with its closely connected relaxation of effort, is preparing us, it may be, for a great fall; at least we are failing to prepare for the moment when we "enter into temptation." For doesn't it all mean—this hopelessness and despondency—that faith is growing weak, and that we are depending more and more on a single strand of what should be the closely twisted cord of Faith and Hope and Love? A loss of hope means a weakening of faith, and a weak faith means an imperfect love.

And, on the other hand, faith and effort react on one another, as do despondency and sloth. Isn't it so in the service of man? When we hear of all the misery and wretchedness and vice of some great city it seems so hopeless, we are ready to fold our hands and let things go; but if, in some little corner of the great field of work, we bestir ourselves to do what little we may, isn't it wonderful how, with that effort, faith and hope and love grow strong and strengthen one another? There is something lovable even in those who are deemed hopelessly depraved—something which we never dreamed of, something we can believe in, something which has in it a seed of hope, and we know that the effort is not lost; that while God is blessing our work among those He loves, He is pouring down showers of blessings on the worker himself, and giving him new faith and hope and love towards God and man.

Surely, brethren, sloth and the unwillingness to make the effort, intellectual and moral, which is necessary for a real hold of truth, is largely to blame for what is vaguely called unbelief, in these days of ours. We know that sin blinds the eye to the vision of God; but do we not too readily forget that there is an intellectual as well as a moral sloth? See how hard we work if we would be philosophers, or historians, or men of science, or critics. We glory in the fact that we live in an intellectual age, and we know that the penalty we pay for it is that, if we are to hold our own, we cannot afford to sit intellectually dle. And yet how few Christians, in this great Minster, spend any time in trying to understand what they profess to believe! to see it in its rational connection! to learn how it won its triumphs in an age certainly not less intellectual than our own! If there is an ignorance which is inexcusable, it is certainly the ignorance of reasoning men, who do not care to make real what they profess to believe. They are keen and vigilant and energetic in business or in secular study; but when the vision of God is before them they are heavy with sleep, and when the great struggle is at hand, and the betrayer is near Christ finds them asleep again; and the first shock of hostile criticism, the first difficulty of the clever objector, which may have been met and refuted, though they do not know it, again and again, seems fatal to their faith, and as the traitor draws near to the Master they have loved, they forsake Him, and flee.

Yet they really loved their Lord once—really forsook all for Him once; but, almost without knowing it, they adopted the world's views of success, and slowly and unwillingly they had to admit the failure of Christianity. And their effort was relaxed, and self-discipline grew irksome, and energy dissipated itself in external forms, and drowsiness crept over their spiritual sight, and at last they slept while their Lord was being betrayed, and then—then they forsook Him, and fled. It seemed so impossible once. Yet such is the power of intellectual sloth.

Can we better gather up our thoughts on this desertion of Christ by His Disciples than in those words of His to them in the Garden, "*Watch and pray*"? If the moral struggle is what it ever was for those who would live the Christ-like life, the intellectual struggle was never keener than it is for us now. And we are quite wrong to suppose that the battle can be fought out for us. Every thinking man and woman must take his part or hers, must fight for Christ, or, like the slothful sleepers in the Garden, look on while the traitor betrays, and the enemies assail the Master they claim to love. If the Disciples sleep, the traitor is awake, the enemies are collecting their forces. Our duty, the imperative duty for thinking men and women, is to make real to themselves, in life and thought, that spiritual truth, be it much or little, which God has revealed to them. The faith which gives way before the sudden shock of difficulties is an unreasoned and unreasoning faith, or it is a faith that was too weak to struggle, too careless to endure hardness, too slothful to watch and pray.

III.

THE DENIAL.

"I know not the Man."—S. MATT. xxvi. 74.

IT is a remarkable thing that, in the Gospel narrative, two of the Disciples, and two only, are spoken of as having been in some special way exposed to the assaults of Satan. The one was Judas the traitor; the other that Disciple who, on any view we may take of the words, was singled out for special honour by the Lord—S. PETER. It seems as if S. Peter stood side by side with Judas in danger. His was one of those affectionate, impulsive natures which feel so keenly disappointment and failure. Such natures combine the extremes of strength and weakness. Their love carries them beyond and above themselves. It trusts itself implicitly, unreasoningly, and when disappointment comes it is unreasonably downcast and despairing. It is impatient of obstacles, of difficulties, of dangers; but when these are seen to be too real to be ignored, it quickly loses heart.

And here it is worth while to pause and remind ourselves that temptation always comes to us through that which is most natural to us, and our danger lies very near to that which, rightly used, is our strength. The devil, as we are often reminded, is not omnipotent, but he is a good general. He will not storm the walls if he can get in by the postern gate. He will not tempt a S. Peter to covetousness, or the other Disciples to treachery, if the impulsive self-confidence of the one, and the sloth and weariness of the rest, will serve his turn.

It was directly after S. Peter's great confession, and the Lord's words, "Blessed art thou, Simon Bar-jona," that there came that stern rebuke, "Get thee behind me, *Satan!*" The love which could see in Jesus, the Messiah, the Christ of God, could not see Him in the Man of Sorrows, the Persecuted, the Betrayed, the Forsaken. "That be far from Thee, Lord!" S. Peter had won a victory for faith when he confessed that Christ was the Messiah; but he had much yet to learn. He savoured still of earth and earthly ideas. It was he who, as they went up to Jerusalem, asked the Master, "Behold, we have forsaken all, and followed Thee; what shall we have therefore?" There was still something of the old worldly desire for a visible reward, a triumph in the eyes of men. He had not yet learned the lessons of disappointment and seeming failure.

It was this instinctively self-trusting nature, the nature which had not learned to know itself, its own strength and weakness, that Satan sought to claim as his own. "Simon, Simon," said Christ after the Last Supper, "Satan hath desired to have you, that he may sift you as wheat. But I have prayed for thee, that thy faith fail not." It was a solemn warning of that "sifting" which should separate the chaff from the grain, even amongst the chosen Twelve. And Christ prayed for Peter, as He prays now in Heaven for us, not that we may be saved from temptation, but that, in the hour of temptation, our faith may not fail, and we may be kept from the evil one. Did Christ pray for Judas too? Surely it must have been so. Even while self-love was struggling against the love of God; even while the traitorous plans were being matured, ay, even after the bargain had been made, and the traitor's kiss had been given, even till by his own mad act Judas cut himself away from the love of God, we may be sure that the ceaseless intercession of infinite love was heard even for the traitor.

That same intercession, that same untiring love, went forth for the self-confident but loving S. Peter. "I have prayed for thee, that thy faith fail not." S. Peter had to learn a deeper lesson of disappointment—the disappointment with self. All his self-confidence had to be destroyed before he could give his real self to Christ. How hard that truth is to learn—that we may not trust our feelings, our highest emotional nature; that even love for our Lord may fail as long as it trusts itself, and does not yet rest wholly in Him! It seemed to S. Peter as if, of all the Disciples, he was least in danger. "Though all should be offended because of Thee, yet will I never be offended;" "Though I should die with Thee, yet will I not deny Thee." Yet the night drew on, and sleep overcame love, and even Peter could not watch; and when the traitor drew near, he gave way to the momentary impulse of resistance, and then forsook his Lord, and fled.

What a miserable consciousness of failure was there—the failure of love of one who trusted his love so perfectly! Perhaps it was that consciousness of failure that led S. Peter to the high priest's palace. But he followed afar off, and waited at the door without, in the palace. The consciousness of having failed, till we can realize that the source of strength is not in ourselves, is only the cause of new failure. We hate ourselves for failing; but self-confidence is not destroyed. We think to recover ourselves by some heroic act, and we fail again, and fall more grievously. Even while the cowardice of the night of betrayal is fresh in his memory, he rushes into danger, and the challenge comes, "Thou also wast with Jesus of Galilee. . . . Did not I see thee in the Garden with Him?" And he who, in the Garden, had again and again forsaken, now denies his Lord. Three times he denied Christ; and when the cock crew, a flood of miserable memories rushed in upon him. That look of the Master recalled the words, "I have prayed for thee," and the Disciple who denied the Lord he loved, went out, and wept bitterly.

In that hour of sadness and desolation, we can trace again the likeness and the difference between Judas and S. Peter. In the moment of disappointment, when together they had realized what seemed the failure of their Messianic hope, the traitor began to mature his traitorous plans, and separate himself from the Apostolic band; S. Peter, in that same hour, rose to his great confession, "Thou art the Christ!" So now, when the Messiah is condemned, and Judas and S. Peter alike realize their moral failure, the one "repented himself," the other "wept bitterly." What a difference is implied in those words! The one knew but remorse; the other entered on the toilsome road of penitence. Judas flung back the hated silver to the priests, and went and hanged himself; S. Peter, in that sad look of Christ, saw, even in the reproach, the hope of restoration, and he went out, and wept bitterly.

But if we would know what the denial, and the repentance which followed, really meant in the life of S. Peter, we must pass to that scene which took place after the Resurrection, on the shores of the blue Lake of Gennesaret. Once more his love is tried. Thrice, as though to recall the thrice-repeated denial, the Master questions his love. "Simon, son of Jonas, dost thou love Me dearly? more than these others love?" But the old impetuous self-confidence is gone. S. Peter has learned the lesson of self-distrust. He dares not claim pre-eminence in love; he dares not even claim that deeper love which the Master's word implied. He answers, "Yea, Lord; Thou knowest that I love Thee." Again the question is heard, as though the Master doubts, not only the pre-eminence in love, but the very fact itself. "Dost thou dearly love Me?" Again, with the self-restraint which has its roots in self-distrust, S. Peter claims but the lower, more external love. And then comes the hardest question of all—the word which seems to question even that lower love: "Dost thou love Me?" And Peter was grieved—grieved, not with his Master, but with himself, and that failure which had justified the words. But there is no outburst of self-asserting love—only the words whereby he dared to appeal to the Master Himself: "Lord, Thou knowest all things; Thou knowest that I love Thee."

And as the penitent's love showed its depth and its reality, even in its self-distrust, the fallen Disciple is restored to his Apostleship, to be the Shepherd and Bishop of souls, to feed and tend the flock of God. But what of the reward? A crown? a throne, such as in his old days S. Peter might have looked forward to? No, not that. He shall have his reward; the reward that the world counts loss, and the loving heart welcomes as a gain—fellowship in the Master's sufferings, a death like his Lord's. "When thou shalt be old, . . . another shall gird thee, and carry thee whither thou wouldest not." He who, in the past, had failed and fallen, shall glorify God by a martyr's death. This is the triumph of the Cross in human life, the death of self-love, self-will, self-confidence. For this is to be made like Him Who pleased not Himself, but came to do the Father's Will.

From love that is emotional to love that is real, that is the transition which S. Peter had made by the grace of God. The Saviour's prayer for him had prevailed. In failure, and through failure, his faith had ripened, his love had been purified, his hope had grown strong. He will stand firm now; he will go even to prison and to death. For he no longer trusts his love, but Him Who loved him. Read the Epistles of S. Peter, if you would realize the contrast between his character, before and after his great fall. Read them as an autobiography, and in the light of his past history, and they will be full of meaning. Hear him speak of "the trial of faith, more precious than of gold which perisheth;" of the need that there is to gird up the loins, and hope to the end for the grace that is to be given; of the joy of being partakers in Christ's sufferings; of the duty of feeding the flock of God; of the grace given to the humble; above all, the repeated warnings to be sober and vigilant in the presence of the adversary the devil: "Be ye sober, and watch unto prayer," as if there were still ringing in his ears those words of the Master, "Watch and pray, lest ye enter into temptation."

Brethren, is our love for our Lord emotional merely, or is it real? It is so easy to deceive ourselves. For we really love Christ, and we delight in beautiful services, and all the sensible consolations of religion. And we have made our profession of faith. We know but One Who has the words of eternal life. And it seems so impossible that we should ever forsake or deny Him. When the hour of temptation is far off, and the traitor and his company are not yet in sight, and it seems as if our love for Christ would never require us to stand alone against the world, it is so easy to trust our love, and believe in ourselves, to declare our readiness to die with Him, if the call should come. So we feel when we worship in God's Church, or draw near to Him in prayer, and realize His very presence in the Sacrament of His love; but when we go out into the world, we follow Christ afar off, and we find ourselves away from Him, and among those who deny our faith. And they challenge us with the insolence of assumed superiority. "You are a Churchman?" or "You believe in miracles, and, amid all the light of this nineteenth century, you profess to hold the Divinity of Christ, to believe in a Divine society and supernatural life, and dogma, and Sacraments, and everything which modern enlightenment has explained away?" Then the temptation comes. We are alone, and among enemies, and we are not prepared for such a challenge, and we begin to give ground, and explain that Christianity is not so much opposed, as is thought, to the views of the world; that the claims of Christ have been exaggerated and misrepresented, and made more uncompromising than they really are. And, before we know it, we have denied our Lord. And even as we speak, His eye rests on us in sad reproach, and we know that, for fear or favour, we have been ashamed of Him for Whom we thought ourselves ready to die.

Who of us has not felt that burning sense of shame and failure and disappointment, when, perhaps in some little thing, we have been led to deny our Lord? We thought we were so strong, and we have failed. And we hate and despise ourselves, and yet are far from true repentance. For real repentance does not come till the thought of self, which underlies even that self-contempt, is gone, and we weep bitterly, like S. Peter, for the sin.

Good Friday is very near, and soon we shall be kneeling before the Cross, and hearing again the well-known words which tell of a love triumphant in suffering and death. And it cannot be but that that love will call forth from us some answering love. Will our love last? Is it real? Will it stand strong in the hour of temptation? We distrust, and rightly distrust, emotional religion. We look with wholesome suspicion on all that is sensational or sentimental in worship. We know that it will give way just when the strain of trial comes.

How, then, shall we test our love? "Lord, help us to know ourselves!" We cannot trust our feelings; we must go to facts. How shall we be sure that our love is real?

Three things may help us to an answer:—(*a*) Love must be love for a Person, not a system. It must be love for Christ, not for Christianity; devotion to One "Who first loved us." It is the distinguishing mark of religion that it implies a moral and personal relationship between God and man. It is so easy for some minds to become enthusiastic about the æsthetic beauty of religious worship, or the rational coherence of a theological system, and to mistake that emotional or intellectual satisfaction for the tie which binds the Christian to his Lord. But the love which is to stand firm, ay, even if we are called to stand alone against the world, is a personal love, by which "we dwell in Christ, and Christ in us"—a love which, in dim and far-off copy, yet recalls the union of the Father and the Son, and realizes the Saviour's prayer, that "as Thou, Father, art in Me, and I in Thee, they too may be one in Us."

(β) But, then, a love like this will be something more than that which, before his denial, bound S. Peter to his Lord. It will prove its reality by its *moral strength.* It will not shrink from, but will covet, hardness. It will expect and welcome disappointment, discipline, severity. It will be suspicious of the world's approval, and terrified at success and applause. And, on the other hand, it will look for and welcome struggle and effort, and the privilege of being with Christ in His tribulation, and counted worthy to suffer shame for His sake. It will be earnest, sober, watchful, prayerful, ever on its guard against temptation, ever preparing and strengthening itself against the hour of trial.

(γ) And then it will distrust itself, and be trustful only of its Lord; content to be unknown, the least among the servants of God, to fill a little place in God's world, to be thought worthy just to give a cup of cold water to one of God's poor. Covetousness, ambition, self-assertion, all are gone, only when we have learned to say, "Not I, but Christ in me." It is the Christian reading of the teaching of the Muslim mystic—

"One knocked at the door of the beloved, and a voice from within said, 'Who is there?' The lover answered, 'It is I.' The voice replied, 'This house will not hold *me* and *thee.*' So the door remained shut. The lover went into the wilderness, and spent a year in solitude and fasting and prayer. Then again he returned and knocked at the door. And the voice of the beloved said, 'Who is there?' The lover answered, 'It is thyself.' Then the door was opened."

MESSRS.

RIVINGTON, PERCIVAL & Co.'S

LIST OF

Recent Publications

34 *KING STREET, COVENT GARDEN*
LONDON

Crown Quarto. With Numerous Illustrations. 16*s*.

Inigo Jones and Wren

Or the Rise and Decline of Modern Architecture in England.

By W. J. LOFTIE,

Author of 'A History of London,' etc.

CONTENTS.—Introduction—The Decay of Gothic-Elizabethan Architecture—The Beginnings of Palladian—Inigo Jones—Wren—Wren's Churches—The Successors of Wren.

In this volume an attempt is made to unravel the history of Inigo Jones's two great designs for Whitehall, and to elucidate the different schemes made by Wren for St. Paul's. The illustrations are from published plates, largely supplemented by photographs, especially of those charming buildings of the Transitional Period which are to be found in the West country, where the Bath stone forms such a ready vehicle for the expression of poetry in stone.

'We have no hesitation in saying that it ought to be read at once by every man who cares about the architectural appearance of our towns. . . . Mr. Loftie's fascinating book.'—**Daily Chronicle.**

'This new book of Mr. Loftie's is one which possesses an amount of general interest concerning modern architects and architecture in general, and Inigo Jones and Wren and their works in particular, as should make it very widely attractive. . . . It is but seldom one comes across a book so thoroughly architectural written so specially for non-architectural readers, and for so difficult a task it could not, we think, have been more competently fulfilled in every way.'—**British Architect.**

'It is cleverly and intelligently written, and evidences large and painstaking research. It contains much interesting biographical information of the career of Inigo Jones and Wren, and in every sense is a thoroughly readable volume, splendidly printed and admirably illustrated.'—**Birmingham Daily Gazette.**

Crown 8vo. With Portraits and Illustrations. 6*s*.

Recollections of Dr. John Brown

Author of 'Rab and His Friends.'

With Selections from Correspondence.

By ALEXANDER PEDDIE, M.D., F.R.C.P.E., F.R.S.E., ETC.

In March. Demy 8vo. With Map and numerous Illustrations.

Diary of a Journey Across Tibet

By Captain HAMILTON BOWER, 17th Bengal Cavalry.

CONTENTS.

From Simla to the Frontier—Commencement of Exploration—Deserted by our Guides—Meeting with Nomads—In the Neighbourhood of Lhasa—Negotiations with Lhasa Officials—Marching Northwards—Entering Inhabited Country—Country with Stone Houses—The Guides supplied by the Lhasa Officials Desert—In the Neighbourhood of Chiamdo—Chiamdo to Garthok—Garthok to Lithang—Lithang to Ta Chen Lu—Through China back to India—Religion, Country, People, etc.—Flora and Fauna.

This work is the account of the journey across Tibet from East to West of the daring explorer, Captain Bower, during which he went over some 800 miles of new country, having to spend about three months at altitudes of from 14,000 to 16,000 feet above the level of the sea, and in temperatures generally ranging from freezing-point to below zero. For five months Captain Bower never camped below the level of the summit of Mont Blanc. The illustrations are taken from special photographs and sketches, and there are also reproductions from drawings of the extremely rare birds procured, and a list of the botanical species found, some of which latter are absolutely new to science.

London: 34 King Street, Covent Garden.

Crown 8vo. 3*s.* 6*d.*

Faith

Eleven Sermons, with a Preface.

By the REV. H. C. BEECHING, M.A.,
Rector of Yattendon, Berks.

In Two Volumes. Large Post 8vo. 21*s. net.*

A Paradise of English Poetry

Arranged by the REV. H. C. BEECHING, M.A.,
Rector of Yattendon, Berks.

This work is printed on hand-made paper, bound in buckram, and published in a limited edition, which will not, under any circumstances, be reprinted. The publishers reserve the right to issue at a future date, should they think fit, a smaller and cheaper edition.

'Mr. Beeching's anthology of English poetry has one great and unusual merit: the pieces selected are selected purely and simply for their poetical merit, and for no other reason whatever. . . . Type and paper are extremely pleasant, and this "Paradise of English Poetry" is a very garden of Armida—so alluring is it to enter, so choice and varied in entertainment, so tempting to linger in, so hard to leave.'—**Athenæum.**

'That those who walk in the rose-scented avenues of Mr. Beeching's garden will say that the planting has been well done, we cannot doubt for a moment. He has not only a knowledge of English literature which is as sympathetic as it is profound, but he has the critical faculty, without which a knowledge of, and even a love for, literature is wasted. He does more than know what is good in literature,—that is comparatively easy. He knows what is bad, and with him base metal is never offered us for gold. There are not many men who can stand this test, but Mr. Beeching comes through it triumphantly. . . . Before we leave this book, we must commend Mr. Beeching's excellent notes. They are interesting, to the point, not too long, and often enable one to get an additional touch of pleasure from the verse they annotate.'—**Spectator.**

'A very skilful selection, and eminently worthy of its name. . . . Will commend itself to all true lovers of English poetry.'—**Times.**

Crown 8vo. 6s.

From Advent to Advent

Sermons preached at the Chapel Royal, Whitehall.

By the late AUBREY L. MOORE, M.A.

Third Edition. Crown 8vo. 3s. 6d.

Some Aspects of Sin

Three Courses of Sermons.

By the late AUBREY L. MOORE, M.A.

Crown 8vo. 3s. 6d.

The Message of the Gospel

Addresses to Candidates for Ordination,
and Sermons preached chiefly before the University of Oxford.

By the late AUBREY L. MOORE, M.A.

Crown 8vo. 7s. 6d.

The Fire upon the Altar

Sermons preached to Harrow Boys. 1887 to 1890.

By the Rev. J. E. C. WELLDON, M.A.,
Head Master of Harrow School, and Hon. Chaplain to the Queen.

Crown 8vo. 7s. 6d.

Old Truths in Modern Lights

The Boyle Lectures for 1890, with other Sermons.

By T. G. BONNEY, D.Sc., LL.D., F.R.S., F.S.A., F.G.S.,
Fellow of St. John's College, Cambridge, Honorary Canon of Manchester.

Crown 8vo. 2s. 6d.

Why we are Churchmen

Seven Plain Reasons.

By A. L. OLDHAM, M.A., Prebendary of Hereford,
Rector of St. Leonard, Bridgnorth,
and Rural Dean.

With a Preface by EDGAR C. S. GIBSON,
Principal of Wells Theological College,
and Prebendary of the Cathedral.

CONTENTS.

Summary—Churchmen put on their Defence—The Church, Christ's one visible Legacy to the World—Christendom in fragments—The National Church and Papal Claims—The Reformation and the Roman Mission—The Standpoint of the English Church—The Apostolic Ministry—The Church's Witness and Worship—The Church and the Message of Salvation—Helps to Holiness in the Church—Bad Reasons and Good for being Churchmen—Index.

Crown 8vo.

Lessons from the Old Testament

Selected and Arranged by the
Rev. M. G. GLAZEBROOK, M.A., Head Master of Clifton College.

Senior Course. *In Two Vols. 2s. 6d. net each vol.*
Vol. I.—THE CREATION TO THE DEATH OF SAUL.
Notes to Vol. I. in preparation.

Vol. II.—THE DEATH OF SAUL TO NEHEMIAH.
Notes to Vol. II. 1s. 6d. net.
Text and Notes of Vol. II. together, 4s. net.

Junior Course. *In One Vol. 2s 6d net.*
THE CREATION TO NEHEMIAH.

Or in Three Parts, Cloth Limp, 1s. net each.

Part I.—THE CREATION TO THE SETTLEMENT OF THE TRIBES.
Part II.—OTHNIEL, EHUD, AND BARAK, TO REHOBOAM AND JEROBOAM.
Part III.—REHOBOAM AND JEROBOAM TO NEHEMIAH.

London: 34 King Street, Covent Garden.

Demy 8vo. With Maps and a Plan. 16*s.*

Venice

An Historical Sketch of the Republic

By HORATIO F. BROWN,
Author of 'Life on the Lagoons.'

'A bright, vigorous, and substantially accurate sketch of Venetian history has long been amongst the most necessary of our many historical desiderata. Mr. Horatio Brown has now to a large extent supplied this want in a work which seldom makes pretence to original treatment, but is drawn from the best sources.'—Prof. T. F. Tout in **The English Historical Review.**

'The reader can hardly fail to catch some of the enthusiasm of the writer as he follows this fascinating story of the rise and fall of a once rich and flourishing Republic.'—**Manchester Examiner.**

'At last we possess, in this excellent volume, a full and adequate history of Venice in English. It was a work worth doing, and Mr. Brown has performed it with care and judgment.—**Daily Chronicle.**

'Venice holds so high a place in the affections of all who are sensible to the charms of beauty and dignity that Mr. Horatio Brown's excellent sketch of its history is sure to receive a warm welcome.' —**Saturday Review.**

'Although, in general terms, this work may be described as a history of Venice, it has been carried out on so original a plan as to deserve a distinct and prominent place amongst the many volumes which have been devoted to a record of the rise, development, and decline of the Venetian Republic.'—**Glasgow Herald.**

'Mr. Brown has imprisoned the atmosphere of Venice into his pages, has for the most part made her heroes live again, and has brought out fully the poetry and pathos of her wonderful career.'—**Westminster Gazette.**

'Mr. Brown has performed his task with skill and taste; and a picture is presented of the process by which Venice was built up and fell from its high estate, which is at once brilliant and accurate.'—**Scotsman.**

'Mr. Brown's learned and yet thoroughly readable book is published in a fortunate hour, both for author and reader. When he writes about Venice we feel that his sympathy with his subject has given him the power both of comprehending things Venetian and of extending that comprehension to his readers.'—**Manchester Guardian.**

'This is in truth a chronicle which follows out with industry and accuracy the maze of Venetian history. . . . As an historical sketch it is admirable.'—**Times.**

'A valuable and fascinating work, evidently the result of research and study.' —**Daily Telegraph.**

Demy 8vo. 21s. net.

Lectures and Essays on Fevers and Diphtheria

1849 to 1879

By SIR WILLIAM JENNER, BART., G.C.B.,

M.D. Lond. and F.R.C.P., D.C.L. Oxon., LL.D., Cantab. and Edin., F.R.S., President of the Royal College of Physicians from 1881 to 1888, Physician in Ordinary to H.M. the Queen and to H.R.H. the Prince of Wales, Consulting Physician to University College Hospital.

CONTENTS.

ON FEVERS: Tpyhus Fever—Typhoid Fever—Relapsing Fever—Febricula.

THREE LECTURES on the acute specific diseases, being the Gulstonian Lectures delivered at the Royal College of Physicians of London in 1853. An Address on the Treatment of Typhoid Fever, delivered before the Midland Medical Society, at Birmingham, November 4, 1879.

ON DIPHTHERIA: Its Symptoms and Treatment.

CLINICAL LECTURES on Croup and the Diseases that resemble it.

Several years since I collected from the journals to which I had originally sent them my papers on Fever. I now publish together all the papers I have written on Fever, because many of my medical friends have from time to time urged me to do it, and also because all the facts detailed and analysed were observed and recorded at the bedside and in the dead-house by *myself.* While collecting some of these facts in 1847 I caught typhus fever, and three or four years later typhoid fever. I mention this because it was said at the time, 'Before typhus and typhoid fevers can be said to be absolutely different diseases, some one must be found who has suffered from both,' and I was the first, so far as I know, who at that time could be proved to have suffered from both. Dr. E. A. Parkes attended me in both illnesses, and had no doubt about the diagnosis in each case. . . .—*Extract from the Preface.*

London: 34 King Street, Covent Garden.

Demy 8vo. 21s. net.

The Hygiene, Diseases, and Mortality of Occupations

By J. T. ARLIDGE, M.D., A.B. (LOND.), F.R.C.P. (LOND.);

Consulting Physician to the North Staffordshire Infirmary; late Milroy Lecturer at the Royal College of Physicians, etc. etc.

'Dr. Arlidge's work should be welcomed by legislators and philanthropists as well as by the members of the medical profession, whose duty it is to be specially acquainted with those causes which affect the health of the different sections of the industrial community. . . . It only remains for us to say that, having gone carefully through the book, we can confidently recommend it as a valuable work of reference to all who are interested in the welfare of the industrial classes.'—**Lancet.**

'A novel and important work dealing with a subject of great public as well as medical interest.'—**Times.**

'We have already briefly noticed Dr. Arlidge's interesting work; but the importance of the questions with which it deals is sufficient to justify a more complete account of the conclusions at which the author has arrived, and of the principal *data* upon which these conclusions have been founded.'—**Times.**

'From what we have quoted it will be seen that the researches undertaken by Dr. Arlidge, for his Milroy Lectures, and embodied in the volume before us, are, from a practical as well as a scientific point of view, of the most suggestive character to all who are concerned that wealth shall not increase while men decay.'—**Standard.**

'Will be considered the standard authority on the subject for many years to come.'—**Glasgow Herald.**

'This masterly work. . . . Dr. Arlidge in the preparation of this work has rendered a signal public service.'—**Aberdeen Journal.**

'This invaluable work.'—**Daily Telegraph.**

'Few, if any, British men have a better right than Dr. Arlidge to be heard on this particular subject. . . . (The volume is) crammed from cover to cover with most interesting and important information, given with a plainness of speech and a freedom from technical pretence that make it delightful reading for those without a smattering of medicine.'—**National Observer.**

'A book of great value and interest. **St. James' Gazette.**

'The valuable treatise.'—**Birmingham Daily Gazette.**

'Dr. Arlidge has given us a highly creditable and useful collection of material on this important subject.'—**Scottish Leader.**

'It should be quite invaluable. Perhaps, too, it may render a service to the community in its obvious moral—that special dangers on the part of workmen or workwomen should be met by special precautions.'—**Yorkshire Post.**

London: 34 King Street, Covent Garden.

With Maps. Crown 8vo.

Periods of European History

General Editor—ARTHUR HASSALL, M.A.
Student of Christ Church, Oxford.

The object of this series is to present in separate Volumes a comprehensive and trustworthy account of the general development of European History, and to deal fully and carefully with the more prominent events in each century.

The Volumes will embody the results of the latest investigations, and will contain references to and notes upon original and other sources of information.

It is believed that no such attempt to place the History of Europe in a comprehensive, detailed, and readable form before the English public has yet been made, and it is hoped that the Series will form a valuable continuous History of Mediæval and Modern Europe.

Period I. A.D. 476-918. By C. W. C. OMAN, M.A., Fellow of All Souls' College, Oxford. *7s. 6d.* [*Now ready.*

,, **II.** A.D. 918-1272. By T. F. TOUT, M.A., Professor of History at Victoria University, Manchester.

,, **III.** A.D. 1272-1494. By R. LODGE, M.A., Fellow and Tutor of Brasenose College, Oxford.

,, **IV.** A.D. 1494-1598. By A. H. JOHNSON, M.A., sometime Fellow of All Soul's College, and Historial Lecturer to Merton, Trinity, and University Colleges, Oxford.

,, **V.** A.D. 1598-1715. By H. O. WAKEMAN, M.A., Fellow of All Souls' College, and Tutor of Keble College, Oxford. *6s.* [*Nearly Ready.*

,, **VI.** A.D. 1715-1789. By A. HASSALL, M.A., Student of Christ Church, Oxford.

,, **VII.** A.D. 1789-1815. By H. MORSE STEPHENS, M.A., Balliol College, Oxford. 6s. [*Now ready.*

,, **VIII.** A.D. 1815-1893.

Crown 8vo. With Maps. 7s. 6d.

European History, 476-918

By. C. W. C. OMAN, M.A., Fellow of All Souls' College, Oxford.
Forming Volume I. of PERIODS OF EUROPEAN HISTORY.

'Notwithstanding its modest scale, this volume (Period I.) will be valued by all historical students as supplying a real want in our historical literature, and supplying it well. . . . He paints on a small scale, it is true, but his touch is sure and his insight keen. For the accuracy of his facts his historical reputation is a sufficient guarantee.'—**Times.**

'Though on a comparatively small scale, Mr. Oman's sketch is complete and vivid. His insight and acumen in appreciating the bearing of events and in estimating the influence of personal character are particularly striking, whilst his pleasing and picturesque style makes the perusal of his work as enjoyable from the literary as it is instructive from the historical point of view.'—**Glasgow Herald.**

'Mr. Oman seems to have, or to have acquired, the art of compression without sacrifice of interest, as we can testify from a somewhat careful reading of the volume. . . . We have only been able to indicate the main features of a most useful and well-executed work: we look forward with pleasure to the forthcoming volumes of the series, which promises to be a monument of utility and of interest to all students of European history. The volume, which is well printed and neatly bound, concludes with a full and well-constructed index.—
Birmingham Daily Gazette.

Crown 8vo. With Coloured Maps. 6s.

European History, 1789-1815

By H. MORSE STEPHENS, M.A., Balliol College, Oxford.
Forming Volume VII. of PERIODS OF EUROPEAN HISTORY.

'The appearance of a text-book of this period of European history (Period VII.), such as the one before us, is an event which every genuine historian will heartily welcome. To say that Mr. Morse Stephens has compiled the best English text-book on the subject would be faint praise.'—**Journal of Education.**

'We are happy to extend a hearty welcome to this much-needed series, which, if it throughout keeps on the same high level of this volume (Period VII.), will fill up a painful gap in our accessible historical literature.'—**Educational Times.**

'Mr. Stephens has written a very valuable and meritorious book, which ought to be widely used. . . . We may conclude by warmly praising the very elaborate index, the extremely useful tables of rulers and ministers of the Napoleonic family, of Napoleon's marshals and ministers, and the concordance between the Republican and Gregorian calendars. All these are very elaborate, scholarly, full, and precise.'—**Manchester Guardian.**

'We have nothing but praise for Mr. Stephens' lucid, well-ordered narrative.'—
National Observer.

London: 34 King Street, Covent Garden.

Crown 8vo. With Coloured Maps. 6*s.*

Outlines of Roman History

By H. F. PELHAM, M.A., F.S.A.,
Camden Professor of Ancient History in the University of Oxford.

'We know nothing in any language which can match his sketch for its ability, lucidity, and terseness.'—**Guardian.**

'But this is much more than a reprint, since the opportunity has been siezed to round off a lucid and scholarly narrative by many additions and alterations.' 'Its value as a popular manual of reference is heightened by an elaborate list of modern authorities, a copious index, and one or two excellent coloured maps.'—
Leeds Mercury.

'Thus he has set himself to sketch the constitutional history of Rome, and he has performed his task with extraordinary ability. The result will be welcome to all students. We had good histories in abundance, and wars described in a fashion that would have satisfied Mr. Freeman; we had no constitutional sketch at once lucid, masterly, and brief.'—
Manchester Guardian.

Demy 8vo. 16*s.*

A History of the Theories of Production and Distribution in English Political Economy, from 1776 to 1848

By EDWIN CANNAN, M.A., Balliol College, Oxford.

'It might well serve not merely as a text-book for students, but as a standard treatise on the particular branches of economics with which it deals.'—
Morning Post.

'Apart from its interest as a history of the development of economic sciences in this country, as a clear summary of the views of the classical economists on the subjects with which it deals, Mr. Cannan's book will be of the greatest value to the student of economy.'—**Scotsman.**

'Mr. Cannan has produced a thoroughly good book, one that is indispensable to every student who desires to know under what conditions the great economists thought and wrote. He has filled an important gap in economic literature, and has turned the attention of economists to a long neglected field.'—
Annals of American Academy.

Demy 8vo. 5*s.*

Elements of Music, Harmony, and Musical Form

A Course of Study, Compiled expressly for the use of Students preparing for Examination.

By M. I. RICHARDSON.

Edited by GEORGE RISELEY, Organist of Bristol Cathedral, and Professor of the Organ at the Royal Academy of Music.

This work has been compiled with a special view to helping students who are preparing for examination. The desire has been felt to explain everything necessary to this purpose in as simple words as possible, and to avoid confusing the student by the introduction of any extraneous matter, or by a superabundance of technical terms.

The book is in three parts. The First Part treats of the elements of music, and assumes no previous knowledge of the subject on the part of the reader.

The Second Part is occupied with the consideration of the diatonic and chromatic concords and discords, suspensions, passing notes, pedals, etc., and, in fact, all that is generally placed under the head of 'Harmony.' It has been thought best to place all the diatonic chords first, and afterwards those which are chromatic.

The Third Part contains short explanations of the various musical forms, both instrumental and vocal.

Folio. 1*s.*

Technical Exercises for the Pianoforte

By BASIL JOHNSON,

Organist of Rugby School.

Second Edition, Revised. Crown 8vo. 7*s.* 6*d.*

Essays in English Literature

1780 to 1860.

By GEORGE SAINTSBURY.

Second Edition, Revised. Crown 8vo. 7*s.* 6*d.*

Essays on French Novelists

By GEORGE SAINTSBURY.

Crown 8vo. 7*s.* 6*d.*

Miscellaneous Essays

By GEORGE SAINTSBURY.

CONTENTS.—English Prose Style—Chamfort and Rivarol—Modern English Prose (1876)—Ernest Renan—Thoughts on Republics—Saint-Evremond—Charles Baudelaire—The Young England Movement; its place in our History—A Paradox on Quinet—The Contrasts of English and French Literature—A Frame of Miniatures:—Parny, Dorat, Désaugiers, Vadé, Piron, Panard—The Present State of the English Novel (1892).

Demy 16*mo.* 3*s.* 6*d. each.*

Bound in paper boards, with parchment back.

The Pocket Library of English Literature

Edited by GEORGE SAINTSBURY.

VOL. I.—TALES OF MYSTERY.
VOL. II.—POLITICAL VERSE.
VOL. III.—DEFOE'S MINOR NOVELS.
VOL. IV.—POLITICAL PAMPHLETS.
VOL. V.—SEVENTEENTH CENTURY LYRICS.
VOL. VI.—ELIZABETHAN AND JACOBEAN PAMPHLETS

The 'Seventeenth Century Lyrics' may also be had bound in Cloth, gilt lettered, 3*s.* 6*d.*

Second Edition. Demy 16*mo*. 2*s*. 6*d*.

May also be had bound in Cloth extra, gilt lettered, and with gilt edges, 3*s*. 6*d*.

A Calendar of Verse

Being a Short Selection for every day in the year from Twelve Poets, one for each month.

With an Introduction by GEORGE SAINTSBURY.

'An admirable little book; perhaps the best of its kind in existence. . . . We can heartily commend this charming 'Calendar of Verse.' If we had not praised it as a string of pearls, we should have called it a book of gold.'—**Glasgow Herald.**

'Delightful to handle and to look at, delightful to read in. No extract exceeds twenty lines. The purpose of the volume is not that of introduction, much less of substitution, but rather to remind and refresh.'—**Speaker.**

'A delightful volume of keynotes to English poetry by which we may strike a whole world of remembrance or discovery. It will be welcome to all those who, in these over-thoughtful days, are able, like common-sense Herrick, "to live merrily and trust in good verses."'—**Daily Chronicle.**

'The selections have been well made, and any who wish to store the mind day by day with high thoughts nobly expressed will find the book very much to their liking.'—**Yorkshire Post.**

'The dainty volume will be found a pleasant enough companion. It is prettily got up, and the inevitable introduction from the graceful pen of Mr. George Saintsbury.'—**Manchester Examiner.**

'Those in search of a very tasteful gift book could not do better than procure this "Calendar of Verse." The selections are very choice and varied, many of the best English poets having been laid under contribution from Shakespeare to William Morris.'—
Birmingham Daily Gazette.

'The book will please poetry lovers.'—
Whitehall Review.

Royal 16*mo*. 5*s*.

Love's Looking-Glass

A Volume of Poems.

By the Authors of 'Love in Idleness.'

'A little volume of poems entitled "Love in Idleness," was published a few years ago by three Oxford friends—Mr. J. W. Mackail, Mr. H. C. Beeching, and Mr. J. B. B. Nichols—and being speedily appreciated by all lovers of graceful and scholarly versification, it soon went out of print. The three writers now reappear in the same association in "Love's Looking-Glass," which contains the original poems, together with many additions. . . . The volume should prove as attractive as its predecessor, for the new poems it contains are not less scholarly, melodious, and graceful than the old.'—**Times.**

'This delightful volume of verse. . . . All the verse is full of an academic spirit, but it is that spirit in its happiest mood, without a touch of pedantry or artificiality.'—**Spectator.**

London: 34 King Street, Covent Garden.

Crown 8vo. With numerous Illustrations. 4*s.* 6*d.*

The Evolution of Decorative Art

An Essay upon its Origin and Development as Illustrated by the Art of Modern Races of Mankind.

By HENRY BALFOUR, M.A., F.Z.S.,

Curator of the Ethnographical Department (Pitt-Rivers Collection), University Museum, Oxford.

'Mr. Balfour, as curator of the ethnographical department of the University Museum at Oxford, which includes the wonderful collection formed by General Pitt-Rivers, should be a competent authority on the beginnings of decorative art and the evolution of the various forms which are now used in work of that nature. That he is so we can vouch after reading the extremely interesting and instructive book he has recently published. Using the specimens in the collection, he traces out and builds up a theory regarding the development of decorative art which extends from the flint implements of the prehistoric period up to the present. To those interested in the subject we can cordially recommend the book.'—**Surveyor.**

'A glance at the illustrations to Mr. Balfour's essay is enough to show that, short as it is, it is a real contribution towards the understanding of what he apologises for calling "Savage" Art. . . . Instead of inflicting upon us his ideas on Art, which might or might not have commended themselves to us, he confines himself to that which he knows, and the result is a most interesting and suggestive little book.'—**Art Journal.**

'A very suggestive essay upon the origin and development of decorative art as illustrated by the art of modern races of mankind, from the competent pen of the curator of the Pitt-Rivers collection at Oxford. It is in fact an introduction to the comparative and scientific study of æsthetics, based upon facts and not upon theory or sentiment. . . . No one has better opportunities for supplying the defect in the scientific treatment of æsthetics than the curator of the Pitt-Rivers collections.'—**Times.**

'Mr. Balfour's subject is an interesting one, and he has done it full justice. . . . The book is written in a bright style, and is eminently readable.'—**Aberdeen Journal.**

'A fascinating and scholarly monograph, which traces by a direct appeal to graduated examples—beginning with the pre historic drawing of a reindeer found in the cave of Thayingen—the gradual development of beauty and skill in design.'—**Speaker.**

'He succeeds in making his hunt after the genealogies of various forms of decoration remarkably interesting to the general reader, and his deductions are doubtless of no little scientific value. All those who are interested in the subject should read the book for themselves.'—**Scottish Leader.**

Crown 8vo. 7*s.* 6*d.*

The Art Teaching of John Ruskin

By W. G. COLLINGWOOD, M.A.

Crown 8vo. With Illustrations. 5*s.*

The Dawn of Art in the Ancient World

An Archæological Sketch.

By WILLIAM MARTIN CONWAY.

Sometime Roscoe Professor of Art in University College, Liverpool, Victoria University.

Crown 8vo. 7*s.* 6*d.*

With Frontispiece and Thirty Illustrations in the Text.

Architecture, Mysticism, and Myth

An Essay in Comparative Architecture, being an Inquiry as to the Basis of certain Ideas common to the Sacred Buildings of many Lands.

By W. R. LETHABY.

Super Royal 4to, 324 *pp.* £3, 3*s. net.*

With One Hundred and Fifty Illustrations, of which Sixty are Full-Page, and Six Photogravure Plates.

English Pen Artists of To-day

Examples of their Work, with some Criticisms and Appreciations.

By CHARLES G. HARPER.

The English edition of this book is limited to 500 copies, and will not, under any circumstances, be reprinted in any form. Twenty-five numbered and signed copies only are issued in a special form, the illustrations hand printed upon Japanese paper and mounted. The binding of these copies is in half morocco, and the price Ten Guineas.

Crown 8vo. 6*s.*

Outlines of British Colonisation

By the Rev. WILLIAM PARR GRESWELL, M.A.

Author of 'Our South African Empire,' 'A History of the Dominion of Canada,' and 'Geography of Africa South of the Zambesi,' etc.

With an Introduction by the Right Hon. LORD BRASSEY, K.C.B.

Contents.—The West Indies—Newfoundland—The Dominion of Canada—The West African Settlements—The South African Colonies—The Australasian Colonies—New Zealand—The Islands of the Pacific and Fiji—Ceylon and the Maldive Archipelago—Mauritius—Hong Kong—Appendices of Facts and Figures—Index.

Crown 8vo. 9*s. net.* *With Illustrations.*
Third Edition, Revised and Enlarged.

Health at School

Considered in its Mental, Moral, and Physical Aspects.

By CLEMENT DUKES, M.D., B.S.Lond.,
Member of the Royal College of Physicians of London;
Physician to Rugby School;
Senior Physician to the Hospital of St. Cross, Rugby;
Howard Medallist of the Royal Statistical Society of London.

Crown 8vo. 5*s*.

With Maps and Illustrations.

Norway and the Norwegians

By C. F. KEARY, M.A., F.S.A.

CONTENTS.—The Land—The People—Seafaring—The Edda and its Mythology—The Sagas—History—Modern Norway—Norse Literature—The Wild Flowers of Norway—Genealogical Tables—Index.

Crown 8vo. 3*s*. 6*d*.

With a Map.

The Forest Cantons of Switzerland

Luzern, Schwyz, Uri, Unterwalden.

By J. SOWERBY, M.A.

CONTENTS.—Introduction—Topography and Characteristics—Political History—Constitutional History—Subject and Protected Lands—Ecclesiastical History—Economical Condition, Trade, etc.—Manners and Customs—Language and Dialects—Legends, Poetry, Literature, Art, etc.—Remarkable Men—Geology, Fauna, Flora, etc.—Canton and Town of Lucerne—Lake of Lucerne—Rigi and Pilatus—Schwyz: the Fortress of the Lands—Canton Uri—St. Gotthard—Canton Unterwalden—Alpine Exploration—Local Traditions—Index.

Royal 8vo. 21*s. net.*

With 73 *Illustrations by the Author.*

Rambles round Rugby

By ALFRED RIMMER.

With an Introductory Chapter on Rugby School
by the REV. W. H. PAYNE SMITH.

Two Volumes. Crown 8vo. 7s. 6d. each. Sold separately.

France of To-day

A Survey, Comparative and Retrospective.

By M. BETHAM EDWARDS,
Officier de L'Instruction Publique de France.
Editor of Arthur Young's 'Travels in France.'

'Your excellent work, "France of To-day," fulfils my highest expectations. It is in every way worthy of your high reputation as our first living authority on France.'—Mr. FREDERIC HARRISON.

'No living English writer, perhaps no living French writer, has a more intimate acquaintance than Miss Betham Edwards with France and the French. Like Arthur Young in the last century, she has wandered throughout the whole length and breadth of the country, and she adds to that writer's faculty of observation, broader sympathies and a greater range of intellectual cultivation. Her "France of To-day" is a delightful book, setting forth the French peasant and the French bourgeois as they are, naught extenuating nor aught setting down in malice.'—**Daily News.**

'The author is chiefly concerned with the France of the Republic; and within a short space she gives us a description which is undeniably interesting and readable, and can hardly fail, so far as it goes, to be instructive. A more elaborate work might convey more information, but not in a more attractive shape.'—
St. James' Gazette.

'Undoubtedly a work inspired by a happy idea. Miss Betham Edwards styles her book "a survey, comparative and retrospective," and such it is, in the widest acceptation of the term.'—**Saturday Review.**

'Miss Betham Edwards knows more of rural life in France than probably does any other Englishwoman. The present volume describes the South-West, the South, and the East of France. No one interested in agriculture and industry will regret taking it as a companion there. We look forward eagerly to the volume which will complete the work.'—**Academy.**

'The characteristics of rural France, and the simplicity and strength which pervade the popular interpretation of life and duty, are charmingly indicated in these pages, and pessimists who profess to be in despair of human progress, will find not a little in this calm and philosophic survey of the social problem in modern France, to disarm their fears.'—**Leeds Mercury.**

'The tourist, the student of certain economical problems, and the general reader, will all find the book worth their attention.'—**Yorkshire Post.**

Crown 8vo. 6s.

A Guide to Greek Tragedy

For English Readers.

By the Rev. L. CAMPBELL, LL.D.,
Emeritus Professor of Greek in the University of St. Andrews.

Crown 8vo. 4s. 6d.

The French Wars of Religion

Their Political Aspects.

By EDWARD ARMSTRONG, M.A.,
Fellow, Lecturer, and Senior Bursar of Queen's College, Oxford.

One Volume. 8vo. 18s. net.

The Iliad of Homer

Translated into English Prose by JOHN PURVES, M.A.,
Late Fellow of Balliol College, Oxford.
With an Introduction by EVELYN ABBOTT, LL.D.,
Fellow and Tutor of Balliol College, Oxford.

Crown 8vo. 6s.

A Short History of Greek Philosophy

For Students and General Readers.

By JOHN MARSHALL, M.A. Oxon., LL.D. Edin.,
Rector of the Royal High School, Edinburgh, formerly Professor of Classical Literature and Philosophy in the Yorkshire College, Leeds.

London: 34 King Street, Covent Garden.

Second Edition. Demy 8vo. 2s. 6d.

High and Low Church

By LORD NORTON.

Being a Discussion relating to Differences of Views within the Church of England as to matters connected with its Doctrine and Practice.

Crown 8vo. 5s.

Things Old and New

Sermons and Papers.

By the Rev. G. H. FOWLER,
Late Principal of the Clergy School, Leeds.

With a Preface by the Rev. DR. TALBOT, Vicar of Leeds.

Crown 8vo. 6s.

The Religion of Humanity

And other Poems.

By ANNIE MATHESON.

Demy 16mo. 3s.

My Book of Songs and Sonnets

By MAUDE EGERTON KING.

Twelfth Thousand. Fcap 8vo. 1s. 6d.

Popular Lessons on Cookery

By MRS. BOYD CARPENTER.

Crown 8vo. 7s. 6d.

Studies in Secondary Education

Edited by ARTHUR H. D. ACLAND, M.P.,
Vice-President of the Council of Education;
and
H. LLEWELLYN SMITH, M.A., B.Sc.,

With an Introduction by the Right Hon. JAMES BRYCE, M.P.,
Chancellor of the Duchy of Lancaster.

Published under the Auspices of the National Association
for the promotion of Technical and Secondary Education.

Crown 8vo. 5s.

Teachers' Guild Addresses, and the Registration of Teachers

By S. S. LAURIE, LL.D.
Professor of the Theory, History, and Art of Education
in the University of Edinburgh.

CONTENTS.—The Philosophy of Mind, and the Training of Teachers—Theory, and the Curriculum of Secondary Schools—Method, and the Sunday School Teacher—Montaigne, the Rationalist—Roger Ascham, the Humanist—Comenius, the Encyclopædist and Founder of Method—The Schoolmaster and University (Day) Training Colleges—Selection from Evidence given before a Select Parliamentary Committee on a Teachers' Registration and Organisation Bill—Report of Select Committee of the House of Commons.

Crown 8vo. 7s. 6d.

Thirteen Essays on Education

Edited by the Hon. and Rev. E. LYTTELTON, M.A.,
Head Master of Haileybury College.